FRANK LLOYD WRIGHT FOR KIDS

CURRICULUM LIBRARY

KATHLEEN THORNE-THOMSEN

Library of Congress Cataloging-in-Publication Data

Thorne-Thomsen, Kathleen.
Frank Lloyd Wright for Kids / Kathleen Thorne-Thomsen. — 1st ed.
p. cm.
Includes bibliographical references.
ISBN 1-55652-207-X : $14.95
1. Wright, Frank Lloyd, 1867–1959—Juvenile literature. 2. Architects—United States—Biography—Juvenile literature. 3. Learning by discovery—Juvenile literature. 4. Perceptual learning—Juvenile literature. [1. Wright, Frank Lloyd, 1867–1959. 2. Architects. 3. Architecture.] I. Title.
NA737.W7T56 1994
720'.92—dc20 93-38150
[B] CIP
AC

The author and publisher disclaim all liability incurred in connection with the use of the information contained in this book.

© 1994 by Kathleen Thorne-Thomsen
All rights reserved
First edition

Published by Chicago Review Press, Incorporated
814 North Franklin Street, Chicago, Illinois, 60610

ISBN: 1-55652-207-X

Printed in Hong Kong

5 4 3 2 1

This book is dedicated to Linda Peters and the following friends who generously contributed time and effort to the project: Resa Baratta, Linda Brownridge, Terry Dunnahoo, Lee Estes, Carla Fantozzi, James Hamlin, Carolyn and Brian Helsper, Donald Hoffmann, Steve and Lucy Howell, Meg Klinkow, Jennifer Koury, Sherrill Kushner, Zeva LaHorgue, Sara Larsen, Trudy Lucas, Viola McDonald, Bruce Montgomery, Carly and Hollace Mulliken, Mark Nay, Alexis O'Neill, Graham and James Pulliam, James Pulliam, FAIA, Jerry Robin, Carlos Roman, Alan Schaefer, Elizabeth Schulte, Julius Shulman, Setsko Takemura, Crombie Taylor, FAIA, Amy Teschner, Diana Wagner, Alicia Wilson, and Gretchen Woelfle.

Photo and illustration credits appear on page 138.

Curr
NA
737
.W7
T56
1994

CONTENTS

7-25-96 Midwest SEO JM 14.51

Glossary

abstract Art that uses only lines, colors, and geometric shapes. The objects in an abstract painting do not look the way they do in real life. The artist draws them his or her own way and doesn't worry about whether they will look the way they do in a photograph.

balcony A platform that sticks out from a building. Balconies are surrounded by railings for safety.

bay window A group of three or more windows that form a space extending out from a wall of a room.

cantilever A free horizontal piece, such as a tree branch, that projects away from a support, such as a tree trunk.

Chicago School A new style of architecture that was developed by several Chicago architects in the late 1800s. These architects used steel skeleton construction of skyscraper office buildings. Their designs were simple, not fancy.

classical style A style inspired by the architecture of ancient Greece and Rome.

draftsman or draftswoman A person who draws plans and designs for buildings.

druid priests Singing storytellers who were the religious men of the ancient Celts who lived in the British Isles.

1893 World's Fair Countries from all around the world built pavilions on a special fairground in Chicago. The countries displayed their latest accomplishments in science and manufacturing.

free-standing wall A wall that is not attached to anything at the top.

gable

A HOUSE WITH A GABLE ROOF

geometry The branch of mathematics that studies shapes in space. Geometry that deals with two-dimensional figures drawn on a flat surface is "plane" geometry. Geometry that deals with three-dimensional figures that have length, width, and thickness is "solid" geometry.

"gingerbread" The fancy cut-out decorations used on Victorian-style houses.

hearth The part of the floor where a fire is made. When the hearth is in a building, the structure above it is called a fireplace.

hexagon A polygon with six sides.

inglenook A corner place where you can sit next to a fireplace.

insulation A material that prevents the movement of heat.

organic An approach to architecture and design inspired by the harmony of shapes, colors, and patterns found in nature.

polygon A plane geometry shape, such as a square, formed by straight lines called sides. Most polygons are named by the number of sides they have. The prefix "penta" added to "gon" refers to a polygon having five sides. The other common prefixes used to name polygons are: "hexa" six, "septa" seven, "octa" eight, "nona" nine, and "deca" ten. If all the sides and angles of a polygon are equal they are called "regular" polygons.

porch A part of a building that is open to the outside and covered with a roof.

polyhedron A polyhedron is a shape from solid geometry that has many sides, which are polygons. A cube is an example of a polyhedron; the sides of a cube are squares.

prairie Patches of level or slightly hilly land surrounding the Mississippi River. Most prairies do not have any trees, and they are usually covered with wild grasses.

realistic Making objects in art look the same way they do in real life. The people and things in a realistic painting look the way they do in real life.

symbols Pictures that stand for words.

symmetry A similar size, shape, and pattern of shapes on either side of a straight line.

tabletop mesa A land formation with a flat top that is surrounded by steep rock walls on all sides. Tabletop mesas are commonly found in the southwestern United States.

terrace A paved area that surrounds a house and is open to the sky, it is usually surrounded by gardens.

tower A building or part of a building that is much higher than it is wide. Towers were often attached to Victorian buildings. When a tower rises to a height greater than the roof of a house, it makes a good lookout place.

turret A small tower that is part of a building, usually round and attached to the building's corner with a winding staircase inside. Turrets were used as lookouts and as places from which the castle could be defended. Castles have several turrets.

veranda A large porch covered with a roof that is attached to a house.

BIOGRAPHY

Chapter 1

GROWING UP

Froebel Gifts.

Anna Lloyd Jones Wright found the perfect gift for her nine-year-old son Frank at a fair in Philadelphia in 1876. Mrs. Wright wanted her son to be an architect, and the beautiful Froebel blocks she bought at the fair would teach her son about architecture. The blocks were invented by Frederich Froebel, the founder of the first kindergarten. He used them to help children understand how big shapes are made from small parts. While playing with the blocks, children learned about geometry, color, and mathematics. Mrs. Wright, a school teacher, was interested in Froebel's ideas and attended lectures to learn more about him.

Frank loved his new toy. There were many different things in the package his mother gave him. He found polished maple blocks in the geometric shapes of cubes, rectangles, cylinders, pyramids, cones, and spheres. He found brilliantly colored, shiny papers for covering the blocks and little green spheres and straight sticks for joining the blocks into simple structures. While playing with his blocks he learned that everything is made from basic geometric shapes. The shapes can be hidden within the outer shape of an object, but they are there just the same. Later in his life he was to say, "The maple-wood blocks are in my fingers to this day."

Frank's family did not have much money. His father, William Carey Wright, was a powerful speaker and a talented musician, but he had trouble earning enough money to support his family. Frank was a toddler when his father took a job as the minister of a church in Weymouth, Massachusetts. While

Anna Lloyd Jones Wright.

working in Massachusetts, Mr. Wright found he enjoyed music more than church work. He often stayed up all night playing and composing music on the piano.

❧ When Frank was ten years old, his father gave up his job as a minister and moved his family back to Madison, Wisconsin, where he opened a music school. Frank and his sisters, Jane and Maginel, shared Mr. Wright's love of music. The family often gathered together in the evenings to sing and play music.

❧ When he was eleven years old, Frank started working on a Lloyd Jones family farm in Wisconsin. The summer work on the farm was so hard that Frank actually counted the days until school began again in the fall! After all, even school was better than working on the farm, where he had to get up at four o'clock in the morning, feed the pigs, milk the cows, weed the garden, and help in the fields. A very tired Frank fell asleep immediately after supper. Twice he tried to run away, but both times his uncles found him and brought him back. The uncles reminded Frank that the Lloyd Jones family had a motto: "adding tired to tired and then adding it again," which meant to Frank that he had to work until he was tired and then work some more. "Work is an adventure that makes strong men and finishes weak ones," they told Frank.

❧ Fortunately there was Sunday, the high point of the week for Frank. On Saturday night he heated water on the wood-burning stove and took a bath in a small tub. Sunday morning he put away his dusty, dirty farm clothes, took his city clothes out of the closet, and dressed for church.

Frank Lloyd Wright.

❧ The large, clannish Lloyd Jones family had built their own church, and Uncle Lloyd Jones was the preacher. When the weather was good the family gathered for a picnic after the service. Frank loved these happy family Sunday festivals. He was free to eat, sing, play, and listen to the stories his father and uncles told.

❧ Life on the farm was not all bad because Frank was close to nature. He loved the low, rolling hills of the Wisconsin prairie. He learned the magic of growing things. He saw the colors in nature change from one season to the next. He watched seeds sprout and grow into plants. One day Frank spotted a red-orange tiger lily in a green field. When he became an architect, he signed every drawing with a small red square that always reminded him of the beautiful tiger lily in the green Wisconsin field.

❧ Frank felt surprise and delight when he found the simple shapes of his Froebel blocks hidden in nature. Tiny green spheres appeared when he snapped open a long, smooth peapod. Pulling back the rough husk from an ear of corn exposed the straight rows of square yellow kernels hiding inside. Feathery green carrot tops showed him where he could find plump, orange triangular carrots growing underground.

❧ His respect for the simple beauty of nature grew with every passing year. Frank learned to see patterns in the freshly tilled soil, in the layering of rocks, in the ripples of water, and in the moving clouds. He noticed the structures of the trees, plants, and spiderwebs. He studied shapes repeated in insects and animals. He learned to see that nature hides the basic shapes of

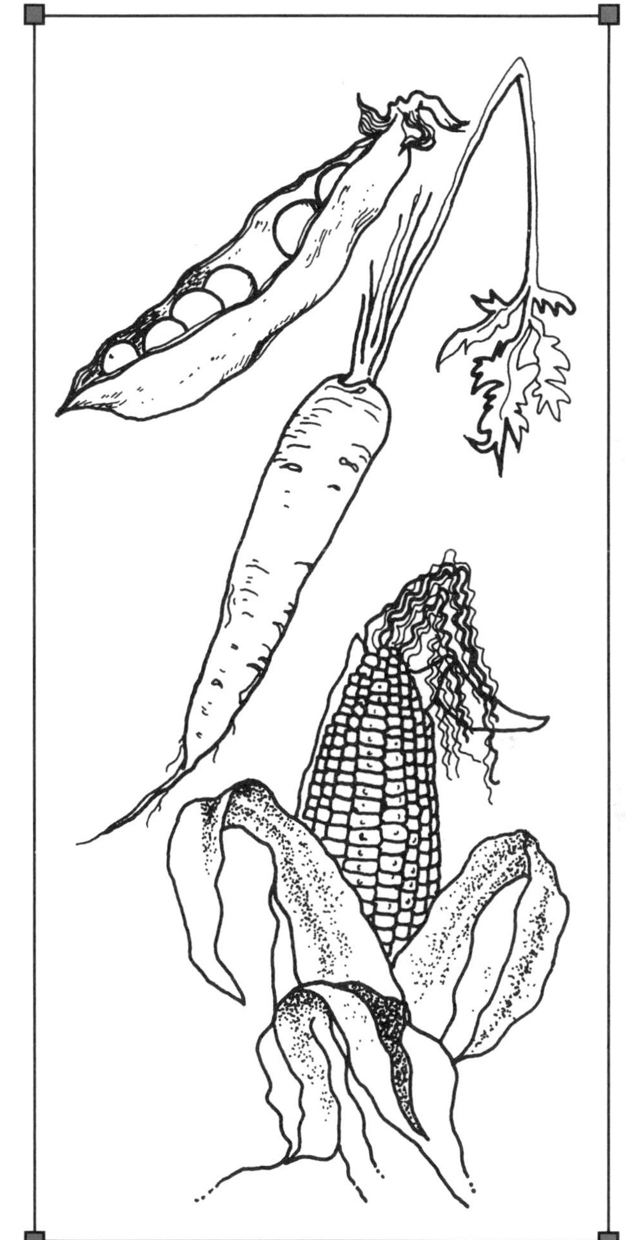

the circle, square, and triangle within the outer shape of everything. This was the same lesson he learned from his Froebel blocks, and he never grew tired of it. Later in his life, these lessons would give him the ideas he would use to create his own style of American architecture.

❧ By the end of his fifth summer on the farm, when Frank was sixteen, everyone treated him as an adult. The hard farm work had given Frank self-confidence and the strength he needed to face the misfortune he found when he returned home. Fewer and fewer students wanted to study music with Mr. Wright, and he had to close his music school. Feeling he was a failure, Mr. Wright left home and his family. Of course Frank was very angry with his father, but later in his life he could at least be grateful that his father had inspired his love of music.

❧ The Wright family was especially short of money after Mr. Wright left, but Mrs. Wright still wanted her son to be an architect. However, when Frank finished high school, there were no architecture schools in the Midwest. Frank's mother saved enough money to send him to the nearby University of Wisconsin for classes in civil engineering, the next best thing to architecture. He found his classes dull, but enjoyed working afternoons in his professor's office where he was able to work on real engineering problems.

❧ The huge dome on the Wisconsin state capitol building was being rebuilt when Frank was a student. One day, while he was watching, the entire dome collapsed, killing most of the workers. The building contractor was responsible. He had given orders to the workmen to fill the supporting columns with inferior materials. Frank was horrified that this mistake killed so many. He vowed to make every one of the buildings he designed strong and safe.

❧ Frank dropped out of school after less than a year's credit. With just $7 in his pocket he set out to seek his fortune in Chicago.

Chapter 2

FINDING A JOB

Madison, Wisconsin, was a small town in the late 1800s.

RICHELIEU
LELAND
HOTEL

It took many hours to travel from Madison to Chicago in 1886. The long train trip gave Frank a chance to think about the fine buildings he would see. Chicago's architects were taking the lead in developing new architectural ideas.

The world's tallest office building, designed for the Home Insurance Company by Chicago architect William LeBaron Jenney, was finished in 1885. He wanted to learn more about Jenney and his fellow architects William Holabird and Louis Henri Sullivan, who had created a special style of architecture for Chicago. Frank admired these men because they were experimenting with a steel skeleton construction that gave their buildings extra strength and made it possible to build them higher than any other buildings in the world.

Because Jenney, Holabird, and Sullivan wanted their buildings to show the steel skeleton construction, they made the outside of their buildings the same shape as the steel skeleton inside. Large windows filled the outside walls and there were few decorations. The Chicago architects felt the height and simplicity of a building was its beauty.

These buildings were the first skyscrapers and this new style of American architecture, nicknamed the "Chicago School," excited Frank. He dreamed of working for one of these great men, and he dreamed of wearing fashionable clothes and seeing everything the city had to offer.

Frank was disappointed when he arrived in Chicago. The city of his dreams was a mess of muddy, unpaved, dimly lighted

Chicago, Illinois, was a big city in the late 1880s.

streets. These streets were filled with strange-looking people speaking languages he could not understand. To his country eyes, everything he saw was unfamiliar to him and it was ugly, dirty, and depressing. He wished he were back home.

❧ However, he did not stand around feeling sorry for himself. He had come to Chicago to learn about architecture and he meant to do exactly that. Since there were still a few hours left before bedtime, he set out to see the city sights. First, he spent $1 to see a ballet at the Chicago Opera House. Then he rode a cable car around the city. Finally, he treated himself to a good meal. After paying for one night's stay at a hotel, he was left with $3 in his pocket. Frank had been in Chicago only a few hours and already more than half of his money was gone. He was worried, but he did not lose confidence in himself. He made a plan: the next morning he would buy a bunch of bananas and save money by eating only bananas until he found a job.

❧ Chicago was growing from a town into a city when it was almost completely destroyed by a gigantic fire in 1871. Because Chicago was the best port on the Great Lakes and the center for the new railroads, the city was rebuilt quickly. There were plenty of opportunities to make money in Chicago and many people became very wealthy. These people needed factories, offices, and homes, and they kept every architecture office busy. There was no better place or time for an energetic young man who dreamed of being an architect to look for a job. However, finding a job takes time, and Frank was short of time because he was short of money.

❧ Finding a job was a discouraging task. Frank was turned down by every architecture office he visited. Sometimes he was asked to come back in a few weeks. That was encouraging, but Frank could not wait that long. He had already grown tired of eating bananas.

❧ Finally he tried the office of architect J. L. Silsbee. He had put off applying there because he knew Silsbee was designing the new All Soul's Church where his uncle, Jenkin Lloyd Jones, was the minister. Frank was in a dilemma. He desperately needed a job and telling Silsbee he was the nephew of an important client would help him get one, but he didn't want to get the job because he was related to the minister. In the end, Frank never said a word about his uncle to Silsbee and Silsbee never guessed who he was. Silsbee was impressed with Frank's courage and self-confidence and hired him for his own merit.

❧ Frank had a job, but he still had money trouble. It would be one week before he was paid, and the money in his pocket would not last long.

Chapter 3

LEARNING TO BE AN ARCHITECT

National Farmers' Bank, Owatonna, Minnesota. Louis H. Sullivan, architect.

Cecil Corwin, another young man who worked in Silsbee's office, noticed that Frank looked worried. Cecil guessed he was hungry and treated him to a simple meal of corned beef hash at a nearby restaurant. From that day on whenever Frank was really hungry, nothing satisfied him like corned beef hash.

❧ Frank and Cecil shared an interest in music, books, and architecture. They enjoyed working together and spent their free time walking the streets of Chicago studying what Frank called an "outdoor school of architecture." They especially admired the buildings designed by Louis H. Sullivan, which were simple shapes with large main entrances framed by gigantic stone archways. Around the archways and at the top of each building was a band of sculptured decoration. The decorations reminded Frank of the plants and flowers he loved on the farm in Wisconsin.

❧ Frank admired Silsbee, but he was soon discouraged by the quality of the work he was doing. He complained to Cecil, "We are just making pretty pictures to show Silsbee's clients. The buildings he constructs never look like the pictures."

❧ Cecil replied, "Frank, architects have to be practical. They need to keep making money, so they build what the clients ask them to."

❧ "That's not honest, Cecil." Frank was remembering an old Welsh motto his uncles had taught him: *Truth Against the World.* "Cecil," he said, "each man must do the best he knows how to do, and not just what he is told to do."

Design for the Auditorium Theater, Chicago, Illinois, Louis H. Sullivan, architect.

When Frank heard that Louis H. Sullivan's office was advertising for a new draftsman, he wanted the job. Sullivan, he thought, was an honest architect. He applied for the job, refusing to speak to anyone but Sullivan himself. Sullivan, who never took time to talk to young draftsmen, finally came out to look at the drawings Frank had traced at Silsbee's office. Sullivan was not happy with the work, but he liked the enthusiastic young man and gave him one week to prepare new drawings. After working late into the night for several days, Frank showed Sullivan the new drawings. He was hired.

Frank started work in Sullivan's office with one definite idea about architecture. He thought a new country needed a new style of architecture. Most of the buildings that surrounded him were copies of buildings that had been built in Europe hundreds of years ago. He admired Louis H. Sullivan because, more than any other architect, Sullivan was creating a new American architecture.

Frank worked hard in the office all day and then stayed after work to share ideas with Sullivan. Often, they talked about William Morris, an Englishman who encouraged artists and architects to work with their hands. Morris believed the shapes found in nature would lead to a new, honest style of architecture. Sullivan explained his "organic whole" architecture where the parts of a building fit together in harmony the same way musical notes work together to make beautiful sounds.

Within a short time, Frank was calling Sullivan his Liebermeister, which means "beloved teacher" in German. Soon,

Louis H. Sullivan.

Sullivan moved him into a special office right next to his own, and they worked together on Chicago's new Auditorium Theater and on a building for the 1893 World's Fair held in Chicago. When Sullivan's clients asked for house designs, the jobs were turned over to Frank.

❧ One evening, Frank and Cecil went to a costume party. Frank, who loved dressing up in costumes, was a French army officer carrying a sword and wearing a fancy shirt, tight pants, and high boots. Imagining himself to be very handsome, he dashed across the room to greet some friends. On the way, he knocked over a tall, beautiful young girl with red hair. Frank introduced himself as he picked her up. The girl, Catherine Tobin, was amused with him and the two soon became close friends.

❧ When they asked permission to marry, both families refused. However, Frank and Catherine were determined and they finally won out. Many people at the wedding cried. They cried because they were happy for the young couple, but they also thought that they were too young for the responsibilities of marriage. Frank was twenty-one and Catherine was eighteen.

Frank Lloyd Wright and Catherine Wright.

Chapter 4

A HOME

Flower planter, Frank Lloyd Wright Home and Studio.

Frank was happy to accept the responsibilities of his new life. He had a loving wife and a good job, his mother and sisters lived nearby, and Louis H. Sullivan had advanced him enough money to build a house on some land he owned in a Chicago suburb named Oak Park. There were a few houses standing on Forest Avenue, but most of the land surrounding the building lot was beautiful open prairie. Frank had designed traditional houses for Sullivan's clients. Now, he had his first chance to design a new kind of house.

❧ He looked thoughtfully at the fashionable Victorian-style houses. He saw they were big, ugly, overly decorated boxes. It seemed the recipe for decorating the outside of these "gingerbread" houses called for as many different ingredients as possible. It was not uncommon to find brick, stone, plaster, wood siding, decorative ironwork, fancy shingles, and colored glass used on the outside of a single house. These materials mixed together on the surface of the house to create elaborate porches, towers, turrets, gables, verandas, balconies, and chimneys.

❧ The big, overdressed box houses stuck out like sore thumbs on the beautiful prairie. Frank wanted his house to remind him of the shapes and colors of nature that he loved on the farm in Wisconsin. He could make this happen if he used building materials that blended together with organic harmony—the same organic harmony he saw in the landscape, where all shapes and colors are part of nature's endless and incredible patterns.

Victorian house.

❧ He also wanted it to blend into the long, endless look of the Illinois prairie. At Silsbee's office, he had worked on houses designed in the shingle style that were harmonious with nature's colors and shapes.

❧ Frank made the outside shape of his shingle-style house simple, like the geometric shapes of the Froebel blocks. He chose building materials that worked together in harmony like the melodies in the music he loved. He covered the roof and walls with cedar shingles in their natural brown color. He used long brown bricks at the bottom in order to blend the house with the earth. He placed windows across the front in a band that reminded him of the long look of the prairie.

❧ Frank's organic approach to his house did not end on the outside. He thought the insides of the "gingerbread" houses were as cluttered as the outside. The small boxlike rooms were stuffed with furniture, flashy knickknacks, and every imaginable kind of decoration. Frank wanted his entire house to be harmonious. Both the inside and outside would remind him of the open spaces on the prairie and the beautiful shapes and colors he loved on the farm. He would join his house together in perfect harmony like a musical composition.

❧ At first, the house was small—just six rooms—but Frank made it look bigger. He used wide openings between rooms, and in places he took the walls completely away. He joined the tops of the windows and doors with a continuous band of wood that flowed from one room to another. He designed furniture with simple lines and joined the furniture with the house

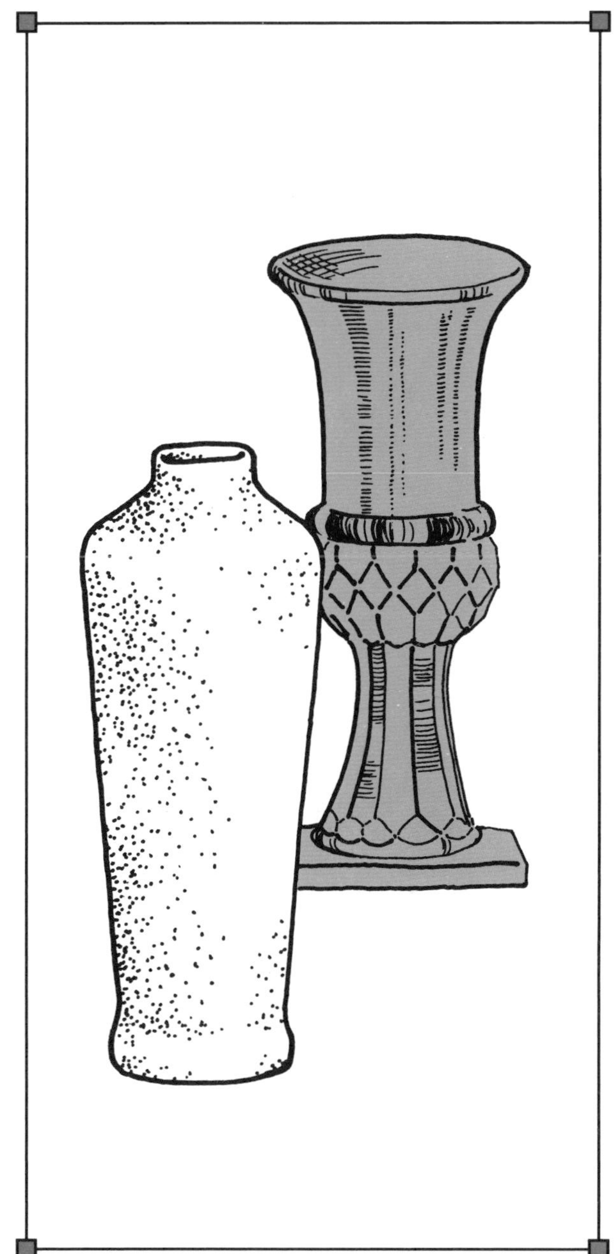

Above: Highly decorated Victorian-style vase.
Below: Simple vase more harmonious with nature.

Above: Frank Lloyd Wright Home and Studio, Oak Park, Illinois. Right page: Inglenook with open space in wall above seat.

whenever possible. He built bookshelves, cabinets, tables, benches, and window seats into the house. Walls and ceilings were painted in the soft golds and greens found in nature. The house was decorated with wildflowers, leaves, and other objects of simple, natural beauty.

❧ Frank thought his fireplace should provide a warm gathering place for his family. It was to be the heart of his house, and, just as a human heart is located in the center of the chest and keeps the body alive, he located the fireplace in the center of his home, to allow warm air to flow through to other parts of the house. His family and friends enjoyed the warmth of the fire when they gathered in the inglenook, a small, private place to sit next to the fireplace. As an inspiration to his family, Frank carved one of his favorite family mottoes, "Truth is Life," over the mantle. Under this motto was another reminder: "Good friend, around these hearthstones speak no evil word of any creature."

❧ Frank and Catherine were happy in their harmonious, organic home. They were often joined by their mothers, Catherine's father, grandmothers, sisters, aunts, uncles, and cousins. In a short time, children of their own were born. The first three were named Lloyd, John, and Catherine. Since the parents were not much older than the children, it often seemed to the neighbors that the house was filled with all children and no parents.

❧ People who visited Frank and Catherine's house talked about it because it was unusual. People who were afraid of things that seemed strange because they were new and different did not like the house, but those with open minds were drawn to it.

❧ Some of them visited Frank at home and asked him for house designs. He did the work without telling Sullivan. Eventually, Sullivan found out and was angry. "Frank," he said, "you must work only for me." Frank wanted to work on his own projects in his free time and he stood his ground.

❧ After working for his "Liebermeister" for five years, Frank left and opened his own office. Although he would miss working with Louis H. Sullivan, it was time for him to leave. Frank had one worry: Would clients continue to bring him work now that he was on his own?

Chapter 5

A STUDIO

Wright family.

Full of dreams, Frank moved into an office space with Cecil Corwin in downtown Chicago. They hoped for big projects like the ones they had worked on for Silsbee and Sullivan, but the big projects did not come. Instead, a businessman named William Winslow had a small project. Winslow thought of himself as an amateur architect and could have designed his own house, but he thought Frank would do a better job. Now that he had his first client, Frank felt he was on his way to success.

❧ The outside of the Winslow House attracted attention. Tile on the sides of the house and strong horizontal bands of brick emphasized the lines of the prairie. Perhaps the most amazing feature of the house was the roof that appeared to float over the house.

❧ Frank built a drafting room in his original house, but his family kept filling up his work space. He solved the problem by building a new studio next to the house in 1898. This way, he could have a private work space close to his family. The office had an octagonal (eight-sided) library and a drafting room with a balcony that was balanced between the floor and ceiling with a clever system of chains and weights engineered by Frank.

❧ A willow tree stood between the house and the new studio. Frank could not bear to cut the beautiful tree down so he left it in place and built a passageway around it. Many neighbors on Forest Avenue talked about the unusual house with a tree growing up through the roof.

Frank Lloyd Wright.

Winslow House, River Forest, Illinois.

In the meantime, the house grew in wonderful ways to make room for the three new children, David, Frances, and Robert Llewellyn. The children needed bedrooms, so Frank cut his old upstairs drafting room in half to make a girls' bedroom and a boys' bedroom. To make the small rooms feel bigger, Frank left a big open space at the top of the wall separating them. The open space allowed light and air to travel freely from one room to another. The children were delighted with their new bedrooms for they soon discovered that pillows, toys, and secret messages could also travel very easily over the wall with no top.

Around the table in the new dining room were chairs with very high backs. When the children sat on the chairs the backs seemed to reach right up past their heads to the ceiling. They felt like Alice in Wonderland in a small private room within a big room.

When guests came for dinner, the children giggled upstairs. They wondered how long it would take the guests to guess the secret of the dining room's lighting. They imagined the surprised look on their faces when they noticed the shadows of tree branches on the dining room table.

It was a wooden grille and paper that covered an empty space in the ceiling where light bulbs were hidden. When the lights were turned on, the grille appeared to be flooded with sunlight. Before dinner, the children helped Frank put freshly cut tree branches above the paper.

Left: Catherine Wright and children. Right page: Dining room and playroom grill.

Above: Catherine Wright, Frank Lloyd Wright's wife.

Left: Their Children.
Top Row, left to right:
David Samuel Wright,
Catherine Lloyd Wright,
John Lloyd Wright.

Bottom Row, left to right:
Robert Llewellyn Wright,
Frances Lloyd Wright,
(Frank) Lloyd Wright, Jr.

Right page: Children's playroom.

❧ For the children, the most wonderful new addition was found at the top of the house. A stairway and a dark hall with a very low ceiling led to a mysterious doorway. When they opened the curtains, they found themselves in a gigantic, sunny playroom. The ceiling high above them had another decorative wooden grille. The balcony was their tree house. They could sit on the window seats and imagine that they were looking down on the world from their own fairy-tale castle.

❧ The playroom was the center of family life, where the children played with their toys, Froebel blocks, marbles, dolls, metal soldiers, stuffed animals, and tiddlywinks. Frank played with his toys, too. He was known to have filled the room with dozens of colored helium balloons and arrange them in patterns on the ceiling. Catherine taught kindergarten classes to her first three children and neighborhood children in the playroom. On some evenings the family orchestra practiced there: Lloyd played the cello; John played the violin; Catherine sang; David played the flute; Frances played the piano; and baby Llewellyn played the mandolin.

❧ Frank wanted a grand piano in the playroom. He did not want to take up the children's play space with the big instrument, so he thought up an unusual solution to the problem. He cut a piano-sized hole in a wall. When the piano was moved into place, the keyboard was on the playroom side of the wall, and the rest of the piano hung out over a stairway on the other side of the wall.

❧ During the weeks before Christmas, Catherine and Frank's sister, Maginel, baked cookies. On Christmas Eve, the children hung their stockings on the fireplace. In the morning their playroom was transformed into a fairyland. A huge tree decorated with ornaments, tinsel, and real candles stood in the center of the room. The stockings were stuffed with oranges, nuts, candy, spiced cakes, cookies in the shapes of little men, and surprises wrapped in funny packages.

❧ Some presents, like doll carriages and bicycles, were left unwrapped under the tree, but the best presents of all were in big boxes wrapped in fancy paper and tied with ribbons. The children would struggle to unwrap the boxes and find smaller boxes wrapped the same way inside. Frank watched with delight as they unwrapped box after box, finding box after box inside. Finally, inside the smallest box was a tiny china doll or a funny mechanical animal.

❧ When Easter arrived, the family gathered budding tree branches and other signs of spring and carried them up to the playroom. Catherine,

Maginel, and the little girls purchased silk flowers and ribbons to decorate their straw hats. Everyone in the family had a new Easter outfit to wear to the services at Uncle Jenk's All Soul's Church. Afterward, Catherine and the grandmothers cooked a special feast. The children played games and hunted for colored eggs and baskets full of fuzzy chicks and candy. Easter was a wonderful holiday. It reminded Frank of the Sunday family festivals he loved on the farm in Wisconsin.

❧ Frank spent his Saturdays at auctions looking at antiques. When he brought a treasure home, he would spend hours rearranging the furniture to suit the new addition. Sometimes Catherine wished all of the furniture in the house was either built in or nailed down so Frank would stop moving it around.

❧ Frank was well liked by his Oak Park neighbors, and he was well known in other parts of Chicago, too. He wore dashing clothes and found endless ways to knot his handsome neckties. He had a wonderful laugh and a talent for turning tears into laughter. People said the party began when Frank arrived and ended when he left. Whenever he had an opportunity, Frank spoke to groups of people interested in his organic architecture. The publicity helped to make him a very popular architect. Soon he received a tempting offer.

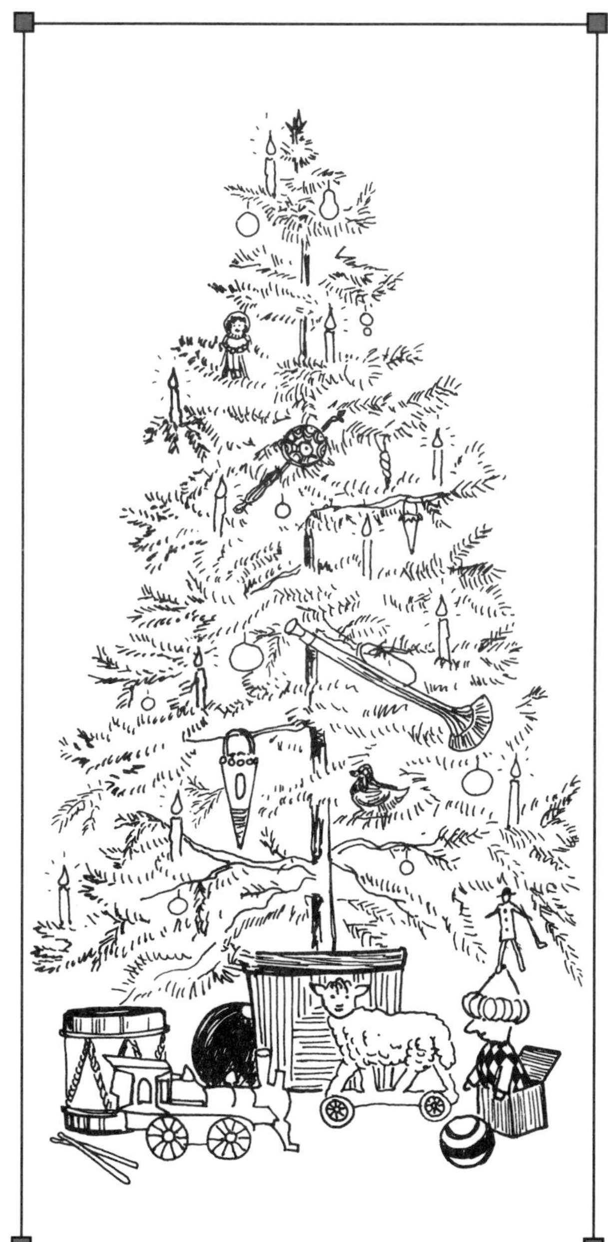

Following page: Entrance, Frank Lloyd Wright Studio.

FRANK
LLOYD
WRIGHT

Chapter 6

THE PRAIRIE HOUSES

Frederick C. Robie drove around Chicago looking for the right architect.

At a party one night, the successful Chicago architect Daniel Burnham took Frank aside and made him an amazing offer. Burnham's firm would pay all the expenses for Frank to study architecture in Europe for six years and take his family with him. When Frank finished his studies, he would have an important job waiting for him in Burnham's Chicago office.

❧ Many thoughts raced through Frank's head. Burnham's offer was tempting, and it would mean security for his family, but all of Burnham's buildings were designed in the classical European style. He remembered the motto he had been taught by his uncles, "Truth Against the World." Frank's truth was the prairie house and an honest new style of American architecture. As long as there were clients for his houses, it was worth giving up security for the truth he found in his own ideas. Frank explained to Burnham why he could not accept the generous offer. Burnham could not understand his reason. "You are wrong, Frank," he said, "my buildings designed in the classical style have caught the public eye. They will only grow more popular with the passing years."

❧ Frank's organic prairie houses had special meaning for him. They were a symbol of the freedom to move around in America's great open spaces. His houses hugged the earth in unity with nature and he wanted them to provide more than shelter. He wanted the prairie houses to provide security and happiness to those who lived in them.

Frank Lloyd Wright.

❧ When Frank designed a prairie house, he remembered the music his father had taught him. The structure in a musical composition is like the structure of a house. When he thought of a house he thought about music. He saw that harmony and the combinations of several melodies in music were the same as the harmony and combinations of colors and building materials used to make a house. He used the dramatic changes that loud and soft sounds and rhythm made in music to make the spaces in his house more interesting.

❧ Although Frank experimented with each new prairie house, there were several ideas that continued from house to house. Prairie houses did not have attics or basements, which he thought of as storage places for things that should be thrown away. Without an attic, the roof hugged the top of the house and pushed out beyond the walls as though it was reaching down to touch the earth. Without a basement to separate it from the earth, the prairie house appeared to be planted in the ground.

❧ Prairie houses were constructed with simple harmonious building materials. Wood looked like wood, and brick was the color of the clay it was made from. The natural colors of the building materials were never hidden under colored paint. Frank emphasized the long look of the prairie by using strong horizontal lines on the outside of the houses. Bands of horizontal windows looked like ribbons made of glass that had been wrapped around the house. The windows were textured with softly colored, stained glass designs that Frank drew from patterns he found in nature.

❧ The main living areas of a prairie house opened up into one large space. The only divisions between the rooms were one huge fireplace in the center and walls that sometimes did not quite touch the ceiling.

❧ The outside walls of a prairie house reached out beyond the house to the surrounding open spaces. Patios and terraces planted with flower gardens, bushes, and trees helped to blend the house with the landscape.

❧ Frank never forgot to design a special place for children in his prairie houses. The playroom he designed for the Coonley family had stained glass windows that taught the children the lesson of the Froebel blocks. Squares, rectangles, and circles all worked together to create a pleasing geometric pattern. Frank even hid a tiny American flag in one of the rectangles as a special surprise.

❧ In 1908, an inventor named Frederick C. Robie drove his new motorcar around Chicago looking for an architect who would share a vision of his

Fire-safe Robie House bricks. Horizontal spaces are deep; vertical spaces are filled in with mortar.

new house. He wanted a spacious, fire-safe house that would have fine views of the city from one large, sunny living area. His children would need a separate playroom with a safe, protected play yard. And he would need several garages for his new motorcars.

❧ Many of the architects he visited shook their heads and told Mr. Robie he wanted "one of those Frank Lloyd Wright houses." Robie's wife Lora approved of the idea. She greatly admired a beautiful prairie house Frank had designed in her hometown, Springfield, Illinois.

❧ The first time Mr. Robie met Frank he knew he had found the right architect. Frank was excited by his idea of a perfect house, and he owned a motorcar that was nicknamed the "Yellow Devil." Frank knew he had found the right client. Mr. Robie was willing to spend any amount of money to build one of his prairie houses. And it was an incredible coincidence that both he and Mr. Robie shared an interest in motorcars. Motorcars had recently been invented, and most people were too cautious to try driving one. The two men immediately became friends of a common spirit.

Mr. Robie already owned a corner building lot in a neighborhood on the South Side of Chicago. Mr. and Mrs. Robie liked the lot, but its size and long, narrow shape presented Frank with some interesting new problems. This piece of land was much smaller than the lots he was used to working with, and it was tightly surrounded by the city. The house he designed for the Robies would have no open land around it. To give Mr. Robie the space he wanted, the house would have to take up the entire lot. It would be a long narrow rectangle that was the same basic shape of his motorcar, the small vehicle that allowed him to travel with speed, comfort, and protection around the city, and also the same basic shape as a huge steamship that allows people to travel with speed, comfort, and protection across the sea.

This was a pleasing idea for Frank: a prairie house shaped like a sleek ship floating in a crowded sea of people. The shape of the house would protect it from the closeness of the city, just as the shape of a steamship protects it from the rough waters. This rectangular shape was organic. As a boy he had discovered rectangular shapes that looked like ships in the layered rocks along the Wisconsin riverbanks. Thousands of years ago, a glacier had scraped a wide path through Wisconsin and left behind beautiful layered rock formations. Many of the formations were shaped like ships made out of stone.

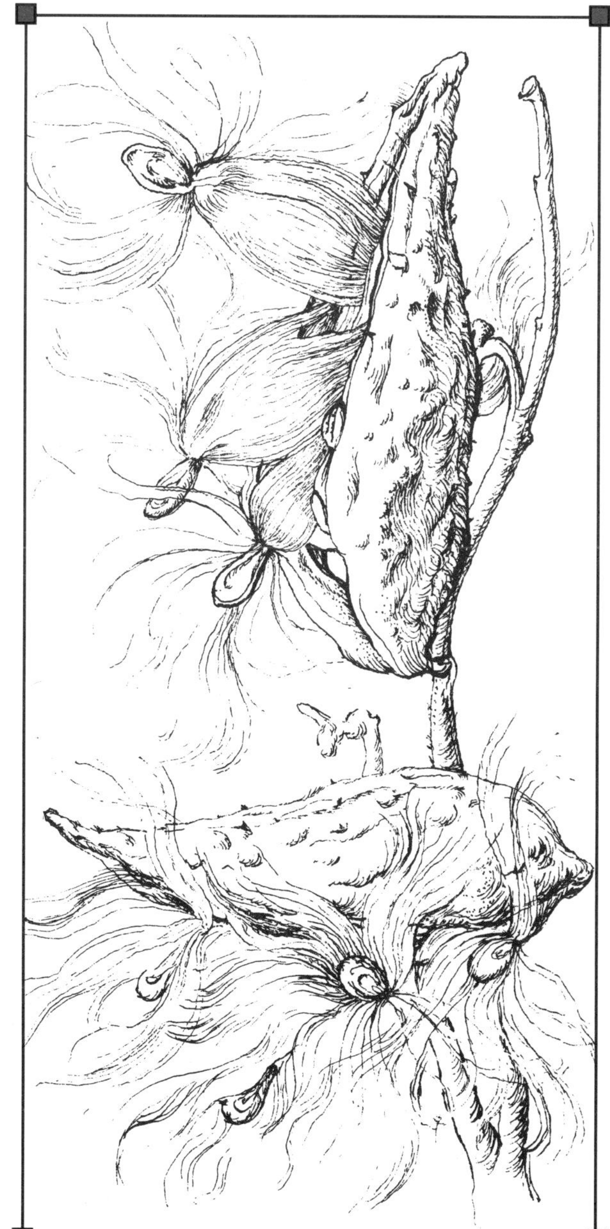

Milkweed.

Architect's drawing of Frederick C. Robie House.

❧ Frank recognized another boat shape on a common prairie plant. Every fall the flowers of the wild milkweed dried up and split open to let the wind scatter the featherlike seeds. One half of the remaining empty seed pod had the shape of a tiny boat.

❧ Frank decided to surround the building lot with low walls to protect it from the city. Inside the walls, the long, narrow house would come to a point at either end like the prow of a ship. Steep stairs would lead from the garden to the second floor of the house. Climbing the stairs would feel like climbing up the steep side of a ship. When the top was reached, it would be like looking down on the world from a ship's deck.

❧ To satisfy Mr. Robie, the house would be built with fireproof bricks and cement. The extra-long bricks would show the colors of the prairie clay used to make them. The vertical spaces between the bricks would be completely filled in with mortar that matched the color of the bricks. The horizontal mortar would be cut very deep to imitate the layered rock formations found in nature.

Frederick C. Robie House, Chicago, Illinois.

❧ A ribbon of stained glass windows with patterns of flowers in soft prairie colors would circle the house. He would draw the wildflowers and grasses showing the hidden shapes within the outer shapes. The leaves would reach out to each other from window to window forming a rhythmic pattern like music in the glass.

❧ He could not stretch the walls of this house out to meet the prairie, but he could bring the prairie up to the walls of the house. Built-in planter boxes would be filled with seasonal flowers. Since objects found in nature are always in harmony with each other, the natural materials used to construct the walls of the house

The windows at either end of the Robie House form the triangular shape of the prow of a boat.

would be in perfect harmony with the flowers in the planter boxes. The flowers would grow up and overflow the walls in the same manner that wild plants grow out of small cracks in rock formations.

❧ He would have a surprise for those who visited the house. It would not have a front door or any other door that could be seen from the street. At first, the visitors would wonder how to get into this odd house. They would think it outrageous. Every other proper house faced the street with its best side, and had a fancy front door in the middle. The visitors might then imagine that a gangplank should be dropped down the side of the house to lead them inside.

❧ They would walk around the two sides of the house, which faced the street. On the short side they would find a walkway leading to a dark cavelike space. They would think, "This could not possibly be the front door," and walk around to the other side of the house. Here they would find large gates opening to the driveway. If the visitors chose to enter the gates, Frank would lead them through a twisting maze before allowing them to find the front door. Or, they might give up and return again to the walkway to discover that the front door was hidden, after all, in the farthest corner of the house.

❧ Once inside, visitors would be in for more surprises. They would be drawn from the dark

entrance hall to a stairway by bright light shining down from above, and they would feel like they were climbing from the dark cabin of a ship up to the bright deck. At the top of the stairs would be one big living space separated only by a huge fireplace in the same way the huge smokestack separates the main deck of a steamship. The opposite ends of the space would be pointed like the prow of a ship.

❧ During the day the space would be flooded with light from the windows, and there would be special lights for the nighttime, too. A multitude of round white sunlights spaced

Above: Sun lights. Right: Moon lights.

Children's playroom, Frederick C. Robie House.

evenly along the sides of the room would give off light as bright as sunlight. Soft moonlights would be hidden under patterned screens on either side of the sunlights. When the moonlights were on, the room would be filled with a soft, dim glow like moonlight reflecting off water.

❧ The windows in one wall of the playroom would come to a point to make the children feel like they were on a small play ship. They would be able to look out through the windows to a protected play yard. There would be a small garage for a custom-made toy motorcar next to Mr. Robie's giant three-car garage, which would be the largest in the world.

❧ Construction of the Robie House began in 1908, and it was finished in 1910. It would be the masterpiece of Frank's prairie houses. Although Frank was pleased with the Robie House, he was restless and discouraged with his work.

Chapter 7

THE HOLLYHOCK HOUSE

Hollyhock House, Los Angeles, California.

Perhaps Frank should have been content. Few other American architects could match his first-time accomplishments in architecture and engineering. He had shown the world his great talent for creative thinking with his designs for the Larkin Building in Buffalo, New York, and Unity Temple in Oak Park, Illinois.

❧ Because he thought of an office building as a part-time home for workers, all of the secretaries in the Larkin Building, built in 1904, were grouped together in a large, cheerful open space on the first floor. Private offices for managers were on balconies overlooking them. A giant skylight built into the ceiling flooded the work space with sunlight.

❧ Frank engineered the first complete air-conditioning system to keep the Larkin Building workers comfortable. He also designed the first fireproof metal office furniture for them. The Larkin Building was acknowledged by architects all over the world as a great step forward for modern architecture.

❧ In 1906, Frank persuaded the congregation of the Oak Park Unitarian Church to build one of his unusual designs. Since the congregation had very little money to spend, Frank insisted on using inexpensive concrete for the new church. Concrete had never been used before to construct a large public building because people thought it was ugly. Frank changed the plain gray surface of the concrete to a beautiful texture by mixing small pebbles with the other ingredients—cement, sand, and water.

Left: Larkin Building, Buffalo, New York. Right page: Unity Temple, Oak Park, Illinois.

❧ He designed Unity Temple to look like anything but a traditional church. The roof was flat, there was no steeple, and it was shaped like the Froebel blocks—two cubes connected with a rectangle. Unlike other churches, Unity Temple was built close to the ground. The congregation could view the sky from inside the sanctuary. Frank felt men and women should study themselves and how they live on earth when they praise God.

❧ More than ever, Frank wanted American buildings to blend organically into the American landscape, but he was losing hope that other American architects would follow his organic architecture. Perhaps Daniel Burnham had been right—it was now 1909, and most Americans turned away from his ideas. They still preferred to live, work, shop, and worship in old-fashioned buildings that copied European architecture. To make matters worse, Frank was constantly criticized by his fellow Americans who were loyal to the European styles.

❧ The prairie house that had once seemed like a brand new idea to him was now very ordinary. He had "added tired to tired" and added it again and again. Frank needed time to rest and find new inspiration for his work. He separated from his Oak Park life and family, traveling and working in Europe for more than a year. When his mother offered to give him her share of the Lloyd Jones family land, he returned to the simple farm life in Wisconsin.

❧ The rolling hills of the Wisconsin prairie inspired him to build a new house. He chose a building site on the edge of a hill overlooking the beautiful valley on the Lloyd Jones family land. Frank was proud of his Welsh heritage and he named his house after Taliesin, a druid priest who guarded the ancient religion of the British Isles. Nature was the foundation of the druid's religion, and the priests were storytellers who told the history of their people in the songs they sang.

❧ Frank remembered his Welsh ancestors when he designed Taliesin. He built his house on the side of a hill just as an ancient fortress was built into a hill with a view over the surrounding countryside. He thought of the four basic elements of nature—earth, air, water, and fire—as he worked on the plans. The stone walls appeared to grow naturally out of the earth. The great open spaces within the walls allowed air to circulate freely. There were water fountains and a stream running through the gardens. He built huge, stone fireplaces to look like the hearths of his Welsh ancestors. He also planned frozen water sculptures for his house. Frost grew on the many windows and the roof pushed out beyond the walls making perfect places for huge icicles to

Taliesin, Spring Green, Wisconsin.

form in the winter.

❧ Frank used the stones, wood, and other materials he found on his land to build Taliesin. When it was finished, the house followed the curve of the hill and was surrounded by gardens, orchards, barns, and fields where farm crops were grown.

❧ He had another chance to find new inspiration for his work when Aline Barnsdall picked Frank as the best architect to design several buildings for her. She had recently purchased a large piece of land, known as Olive Hill, near the center of Los Angeles, where she planned to build a theater, a children's playhouse, apartments for actors and artists, and a small shopping center. The first step in the ambitious project was a large new home for her family.

❧ Traveling through the western United States on his way to Los Angeles, Frank saw a different American landscape. Rock formations and mountains rose up from the sweeping flat desert land to meet the endless blue sky. The red, violet, and orange colors of the sunrise and sunset were brilliant against the soft gold, brown, and green colors of the desert.

❧ Olive Hill, true to its name, was covered with soft gray-green olive trees. From the top of the hill, it was possible to see great distances through the clear, dry desert air. Frank placed the house so it would have views of the ocean, the mountains, and the tall buildings of downtown Los Angeles. He designed it to look as naturally a part of Olive Hill as rock formations are a part of mountainsides. Because of the warm Los Angeles weather, the gardens surrounding the house stayed green all

Aline Barnsdall and daughter, Sugar Top.

year long and were pleasant places to spend time, even in the winter.

❧ Aline Barnsdall was an agreeable client, but there were problems from the very beginning. She spent all of her time traveling around the world. At this time in Frank's life, he was always traveling, too. In 1914, he was chosen to design an important project in Tokyo, Japan—the Imperial Hotel. Work on the impressive hotel continued for many years. During these years, Frank traveled frequently to Tokyo. Frank and Aline discussed plans for the new house in letters and telegrams they sent each other all over the world.

❧ Later Frank wrote in his autobiography, "I would hear from Aline when I was wandering around in the maze of the Imperial Hotel in Tokyo and she was in Hollywood. She would get my telegram in Spain when I eventually got to Hollywood. And I would hear from her in New York while I was in Chicago or San Francisco. Or, she would write to me from a camp in the Rocky Mountains when I was seasick out on the Pacific Ocean."

❧ Aline made an unusual request in one of her letters. She wanted to use her favorite flower, the hollyhock, in the decorations Frank planned for her house.

❧ When the house was finished, visitors saw real hollyhocks growing in the gardens, and they saw Frank's architectural hollyhocks. He had simplified the flowers, leaves, and stem to the basic geometric shapes of the Froebel blocks, and then he had decorated the house with geometric flowers. Cast concrete hollyhocks grew from the corners of the roof. A pattern of hollyhocks was pressed into the plaster that covered the outside walls. Inside the house, concrete hollyhocks grew on the living room walls, and hollyhocks were carved into the backs of the dining room chairs. Hollyhocks were woven into the carpets that covered the floors. Some visitors thought they could even see hollyhocks hidden in the stained glass windows. In fact, there were so many hollyhocks in Aline's house that it was soon nicknamed the "Hollyhock House."

❧ Frank designed a mysterious entrance to Hollyhock House. A dark, low walkway led to a small cavelike hall that opened into a large, bright living space. The high ceiling was shaped and painted to feel like a soft desert landscape. Glass doors and windows brought light and a view of the surrounding gardens inside the house. The four natural elements—earth, air, fire, and water—were found at the giant fireplace. Earth was represented by the concrete stones used to build it. Light and air filtered down from a skylight above. Fire burned within the hearth. A

tiny horseshoe-shaped pond of running water separated the fireplace from the rest of the room. Frank decorated the space above the hearth with a design that showed shapes he found in nature simplified to the basic geometric shapes of the Froebel blocks: the circle, the square, and the triangle.

❧ Frank, who created wonderful playrooms for the children who lived in his houses, made a special place for Aline's daughter, Sugar Top. Because Sugar Top was a very little girl living in a very big house, he made part of the house feel like it was just her size. Sugar Top had her own child-sized bedroom, bathroom, dressing room, and play porch. Frank did more than make the rooms the right size for a child. He created a place in the dressing room that Sugar Top could imagine was her very own private tree house. From the sunny, open play porch windows, she looked out to her very own child-sized garden.

❧ Aline and Sugar Top lived in their beautiful new house for only a short time. Soon Aline discovered that she could not be happy living in just one place. Frank was disappointed when she asked him to stop working on her project. He had already drawn plans for a theater building and construction work on a children's playhouse and two smaller houses for Olive Hill was under way. A few years later, Aline gave Hollyhock House and most of Olive Hill as a gift to Los Angeles because she wanted it to be saved as a place for children to learn about art and the theater. To this day, the Hollyhock House is open to the children and people of Los Angeles as a museum, a gallery, and an art school.

Left: Sugar Top on the steps of Hollyhock House.
Right page: Inside courtyard, Hollyhock House.

Concrete Hollyhocks.

❧ Frank stayed in Los Angeles for a while and continued to build concrete houses. Concrete was a good building material to use in the desert. It was cheap, it looked like stone, and it was easy to shape. Frank showed his skills as both engineer and architect when he invented a way of holding hollow concrete blocks together with strong steel rods. Steel woven through concrete made a building material that reminded Frank of the spiderwebs. Four houses built in Los Angeles from Frank's blocks are nicknamed the "Textile Block" houses. This is another way of saying that the houses are woven together to make them strong in the same way threads are woven together to make a fabric strong.

❧ The hollow concrete building blocks reminded Frank of another object found in nature. A seashell is decorated with beautiful patterns, and it provides a home for the creature who lives inside. In the same way that nature provides beautiful housing for small sea creatures, Frank decorated the outside of his concrete block shells and used them for both the inside and outside walls of the Textile Block houses.

❧ These houses were a new accomplishment for Frank, and he was pleased with them, but, in general, the rest of his work did not go as well.

Chapter 8

FALLINGWATER

Living room of Fallingwater. The hearth is built on the rocky ledge of the waterfall.

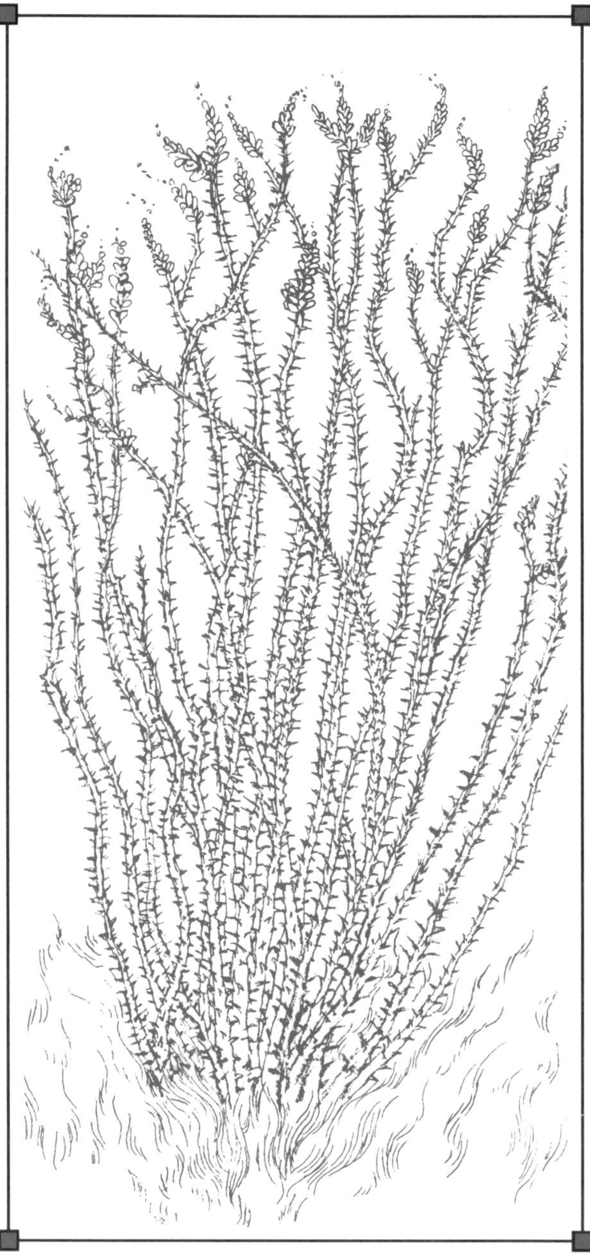

The twenties were trying times. With great hope for new accomplishments, Frank began work on many interesting projects: a huge ranch, a resort in Lake Tahoe, a hotel and elaborate water gardens in Arizona, a 32-story skyscraper in Chicago, a planetarium in Baltimore, and a fantastic 150-story cathedral and skyscraper. Every one of these projects was canceled. Sometimes Frank was not even paid for his work, making life very difficult for him.

He spent one happy winter working on a hotel called San Marcos in the Desert. Frank and his drafting assistants set up a temporary camp in the desert near the hotel. They built tents from cheap lumber and canvas fabric and painted them red to match the desert sunset. When the camp was finished, they named it "Ocatillo" after a cactus that blooms with bright red flowers. From a distance, Ocatillo looked like a group of giant red butterflies resting on the black desert rocks.

When the stock market crash struck the United States in 1929 and a serious economic depression followed, almost all Americans had hard times. The only client for new architectural work was the United States government, and the government jobs always went to traditional architects. Experimental architects like Frank had absolutely no work. During the depression, not everything was bad for Frank. He was invited to be part of an important exhibit in New York that showed the work of the world's leading architects—the Swiss Le Corbusier, the Germans Mies van der Rohe and Walter Gropius, and the American Frank Lloyd Wright.

Ocotillo. Frank Lloyd Wright preferred to spell the name of his camp Ocatillo.

❧ Frank spent the depression years writing his autobiography and giving speeches on his favorite subject, organic architecture. Another project was an architectural school. Frank wanted to train young architects to design organic buildings when America began to build again. His home, Taliesin, was enlarged to make room for students and classroom/studios. The first year the school he called the Taliesin Fellowship was open, twenty-three students came from all over the world. Frank planned unusual classes for them. They learned by making things with their hands. Students were expected to become skilled at many different crafts: woodworking, glassmaking, pottery, textiles, landscaping, sculpture, painting, drama, music, and dance.

❧ Learning to work together was another important part of student life, because a successful architect must be able to work with others. Students were responsible for running the Taliesin farm and for building new additions to the house, school, and barns. Students did housework, cooked and served meals, cared for the flower gardens, and grew their own food in the vegetable garden. While the students "added tired to tired," they liked to sing a song written by Frank called the "T-Square and Triangle Work Song."

❧ As the years passed, Frank grew more and more concerned about the problems of the overcrowded American cities. He believed that city life would be more peaceful if every family had wide open space surrounding them. With the help of his students, he created an imaginary city that he hoped would show his fellow Americans how city life could be improved with good architectural design. There would be no crime, no racism, no political demonstrations, no pollution, no crowding, and no money problems in Frank's imaginary city. Every family would have a small piece of land to farm. There would be small apartments for single people, small shopping centers, small businesses, little factories, and little schools in Frank's city because he believed that citizens who are surrounded by open space and nature will live a happier life.

❧ Frank called this imaginary place "Broadacre City." A model of it toured the United States during the thirties. The model was a great social success because Americans who saw it began thinking of ways to improve their cities. It was a personal success for Frank because it brought him respect from his fellow Americans.

❧ Money to pay for the traveling exhibit of Broadacre City was contributed by the parents of Edgar Kaufmann, Jr., one of Frank's students. In 1934, the Kaufmanns invited Frank to visit their

weekend cabin in Mill Run, Pennsylvania. Frank's imagination was captured by the beautiful sight of water falling over a rocky ledge in a stream named Bear Run. The waterfall was a favorite gathering place for the Kaufmann family because they enjoyed the great beauty of nature they found there.

❧ When Frank returned home to Taliesin he often thought about Bear Run and the music he heard in the sound of its falling water. A house began to take shape in his mind, a house that would be part of nature's music. If the Kaufmanns agreed, he would design a house that would be built on the giant rocky ledge above the waterfall. The rocky ledge would "root" the house to the earth in the same way roots firmly attach a tree to the earth. The house would cantilever or extend out over the waterfall in the same way a tree branch extends out from the trunk of a tree. In fact, the house Frank dreamed of would be like a tree house, which is part of nature but also a safe place for people to live. Frank planned to build the house using materials he found on the Kaufmanns' land. These natural materials would blend in perfect organic harmony with the music of the stream and the other parts of nature.

❧ The Kaufmann House would appear to float in the air above the waterfall. The fireplace would rise out of the giant rock that would root the house to the earth. The four basic elements—earth, air, fire, and water—would come together in the Kaufmann House to show the great contrasts Frank saw in nature: light and dark, earth and air, and fire and water. The Kaufmann House would show how men and women can live in complete harmony with nature.

Left page: Taliesin students loading hay. Right: Bear Run waterfall and rocky ledges.

❧ Frank wrote a long letter to the Kaufmann family describing the house he wanted to build over the waterfall on Bear Run. The Kaufmanns were excited by his ideas and wrote back asking him to prepare sketches of the house. This was the last time Frank worked on the house until Mr. Kaufmann telephoned him one morning at Taliesin from nearby Milwaukee. "I am on my way to see you," he said, "and I am looking forward to looking at the sketches of the house you described in your letter." Frank immediately sat down and began drawing. When Mr. Kaufmann arrived, Frank took him to the dining room for lunch. While they ate and took a tour of the Taliesin farm, Frank's students drew up the first plans for the house. Later in the afternoon, Frank proudly showed Mr. Kaufmann sketches and drawings for his new house. The amazing end to this story is that the Kaufmann House, called Fallingwater, was built almost exactly as Frank drew it that morning.

❧ As Frank grew older, it became harder for him to live through the cold Wisconsin winters. Because he loved the warm, dry Arizona desert, he decided his school could divide the year equally between Taliesin in Wisconsin and a warmer Taliesin West in Arizona. In 1937, Frank bought a piece of land twenty-six miles from Phoenix on a great flat tabletop mesa in the mountains. Standing on his new land was for him like being "on top of the world peeking over the universe at sunrise with clear sky in between."

❧ Because the desert had bold shapes and was very bare, Frank designed his house and new school buildings with sharp

Left: Frank Lloyd Wright.

Fallingwater, Mill Run, Pennsylvania.

Above: Arizona desert. Right page: Taliesin West, Scottsdale, Arizona.

angles and hard lines to match the surrounding desert. His students built Taliesin West with their own hands. When they were finished, the buildings looked as though they had stood in the desert for hundreds of years,as natural as the rocks on mountain slopes. Remembering his Ocatillo camp, Frank used canvas for the tops and sides of the buildings so that the rooms would be open to let the desert air flow through.

In his later years, Frank turned his attention to a surprising project for a successful and famous architect. While he designed many houses for rich clients, he thought about houses that could be built for Americans with an average amount of money. This idea took shape in the Usonian houses. The first Usonian house was built in 1937 in Madison, Wisconsin, for Herbert and Katherine Jacobs.

Since the Jacobs family had very little money to spend on a new house, Frank saved money by making the house very simple. There was no basement. Hot water pipes were buried underneath the floor to heat the house, acting like a giant hot water bottle in the winter. The walls were ready-made sandwiches of building materials that workers could quickly put in place, and the roof was insulation squeezed between layers of roofing material. Electrical wires, plumbing, and gas pipes were all located in the same place. The family car was parked in an open carport. All of these money-saving construction tricks helped Frank build the Jacobs family a very fine house

for a small amount of money.

❧ Even though the Jacobs House cost very little to build, it was in every way as beautiful as Frank's other houses. Like the Winslow House, the first house Frank designed after leaving Louis Sullivan's office, the roof of the Jacobs Usonian House appeared to float over the house. Frank made this happen with a band of windows placed along the top of the walls just under the roof. There was a large fireplace in the center of the open living space, and large glass windows looked out on a private garden. The basic elements of nature were in the simple Jacobs Usonian House just as they had been in the houses Wright designed for his wealthier clients.

❧ Just like the Winslow House, the Jacobs Usonian House became a popular sight-seeing attraction. So many people knocked on the Jacobs's door and asked to see the house that the family began charging an admission fee. Frank designed more Usonian houses that were built all over America. In fact, Frank's Usonian houses were the very first American ranch-style houses.

❧ As he grew older and older, Frank continued to "add tired to tired." He never seemed to stop coming up with completely new ideas, and nature was still a source of inspiration. Frank borrowed the idea for a house he designed for the Hanna family in Palo Alto, California, from the honeybee. The house was based on the six-sided hexagon that makes up the tiny cells of the honeycomb. Everything in the Hanna's Honeycomb House—even the tables and beds—were hexagons or parts of hexagons. In keeping with the inspiration for their house, the Hanna family kept honeybee hives in the gardens.

❧ Happy times at the Taliesin Fellowship were spent celebrating festivals that reminded Frank of the Lloyd Jones family Sunday gatherings he loved as a child. Every summer the students returned to Taliesin in time to celebrate Frank's birthday on June 8 by setting off fireworks and floating hundreds of small candles on the Taliesin pond.

❧ Another Fellowship favorite was the Easter festival celebrated at Taliesin West. As many as 150 guests were invited to join the festivities. Easter Sunday began with breakfast. Tables were set up outside and decorated with flowers and brightly colored Easter eggs. All of the guests dressed in fine outfits, but the women were always the center of attention; they wore fantastic, self-decorated hats. After breakfast, the students sang and then asked the guests to join them in singing Easter hymns. In 1959, Frank became sick at Eastertime. With his family and friends surrounding him, he died peacefully.

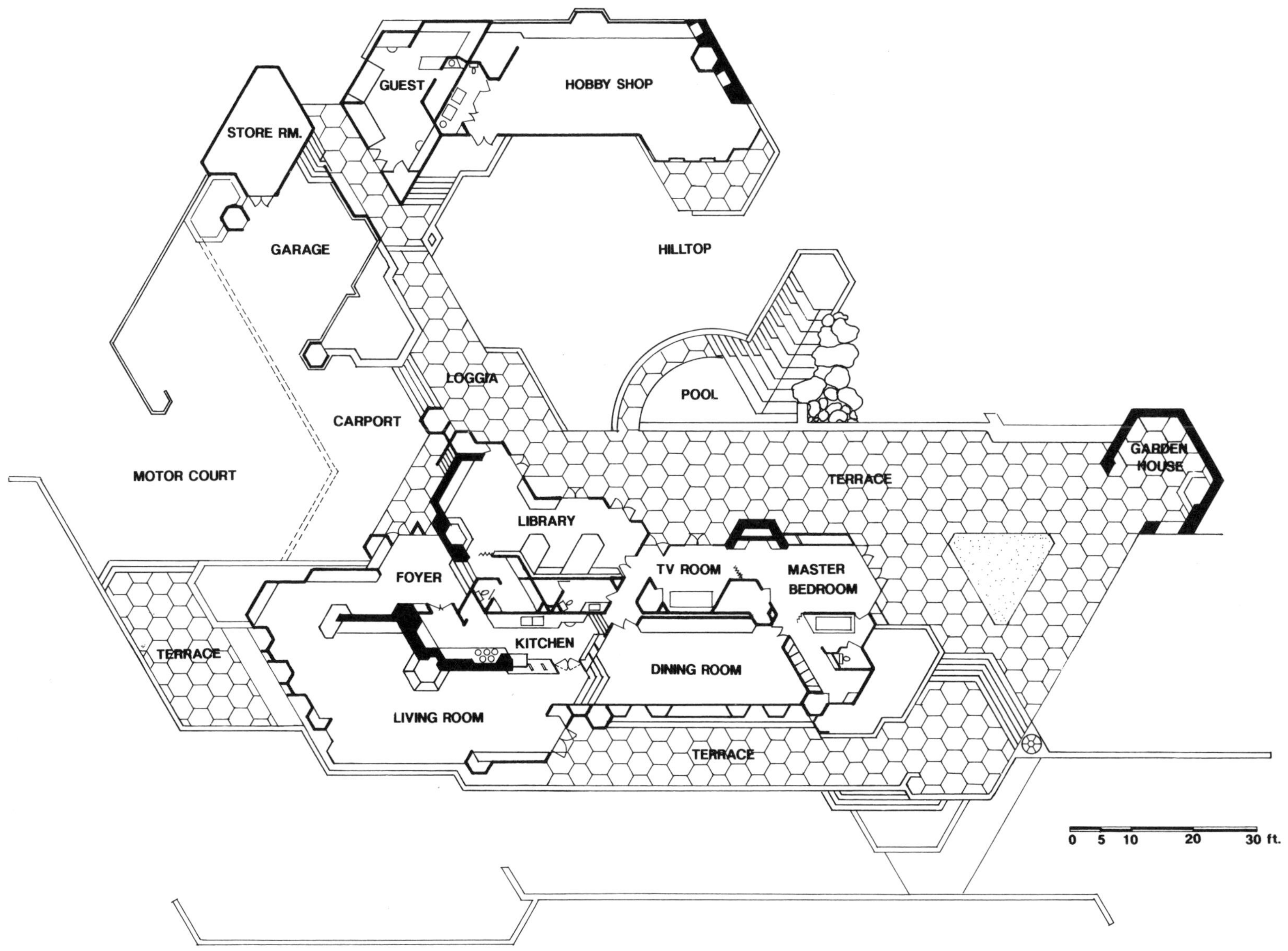

Floor Plan, Hanna "Honeycomb" House, Palo Alto, California.

❧ Frank Lloyd Wright had worked as an architect for seventy-two years, "adding tired to tired" and sticking to his ideas even when everyone was against him. He is called "the Father of American Architecture." Sightseers now travel from all over the world to see his best-known houses, the Home and Studio in Oak Park, Illinois, the Robie House in Chicago, the Hollyhock House in Los Angeles, and Fallingwater in Mill Run, Pennsylvania. Perhaps we can best remember Frank Lloyd Wright in his own words: "We must study nature," he said. "Nature can show us how the principles of form and design are the inner rhythm of all beings. A genius is a man who has an eye to see nature, a man with a heart to feel nature, and a man with the boldness to follow nature."

ACTIVITIES

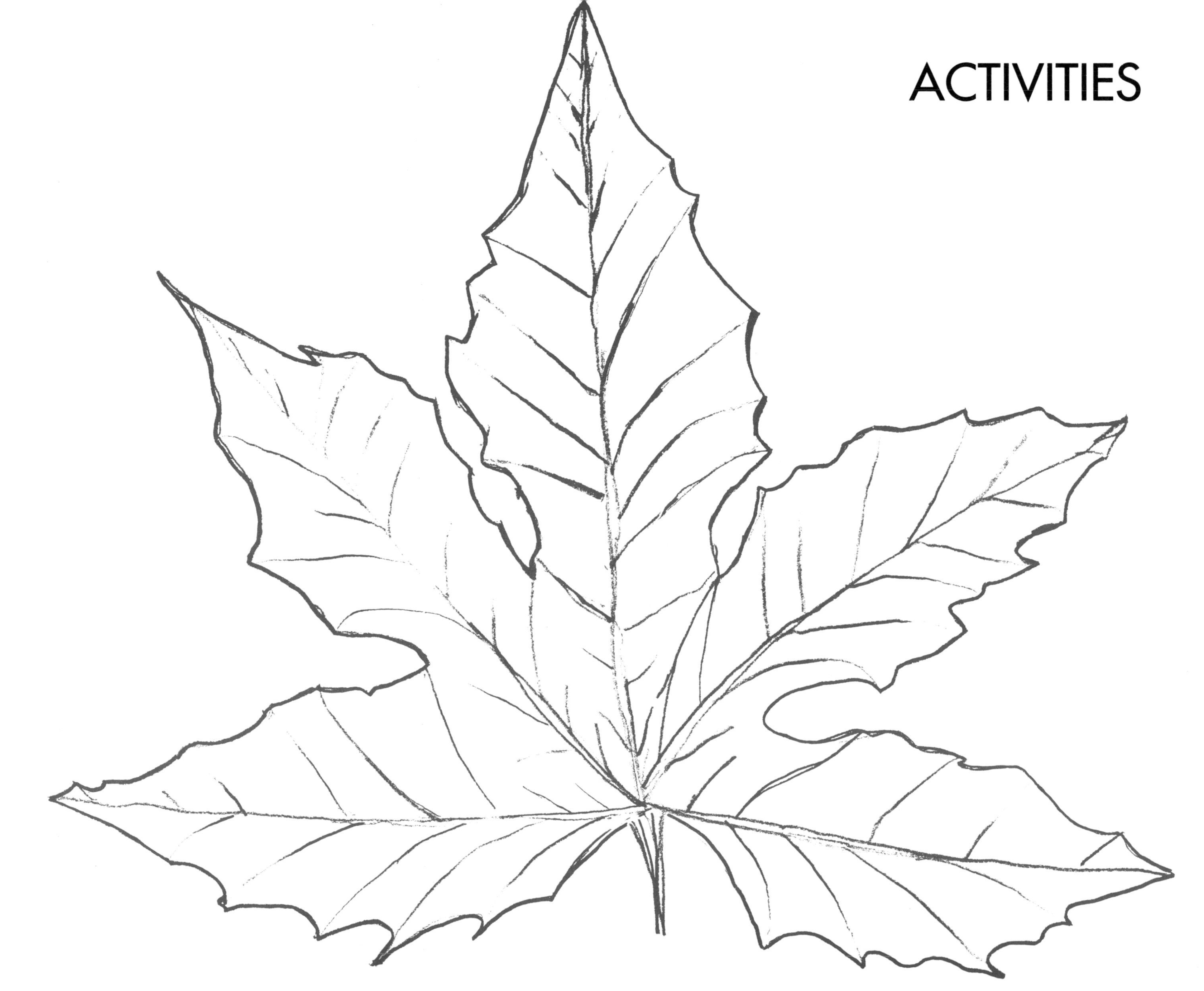

COOKING FRANK LLOYD WRIGHT'S FAVORITE BREAKFAST

Frank Lloyd Wright liked simple foods. Here is a recipe for a special kind of oatmeal he ate for breakfast every morning. This recipe can be made with regular oatmeal, but steel-cut oats will make the oatmeal chewier.

Steel-cut oats or oatmeal, sometimes called Irish or Scottish oatmeal, is available at health food stores and specialty food shops.

Frank Lloyd Wright's Steel-Cut Oatmeal

Measure the water and pour it into a saucepan. Add the salt and bring the water to a boil. Add the oats. Turn down the heat and cook slowly (uncovered) for 20 minutes, stirring occasionally, until most of the water is absorbed. Turn off the flame, cover the oatmeal, and leave it on the stove for 5 to 10 minutes. Serve the oatmeal hot. You may wish to add a teaspoon of butter, milk or cream, and brown sugar to your bowl of steel-cut oats.

Ingredients

2 cups water
3/8 teaspoon salt
1/2 cup steel-cut oats
Butter (optional)
Milk or cream (optional)
Brown sugar (optional)

Utensils

Plastic or metal measuring cups
Measuring spoons
Saucepan with cover
Wooden spoon

Materials

2 small pieces clear glass

Small piece blotter paper or one sheet of absorbent paper toweling that has been folded several times to make it thicker

1 package bean seeds

2 rubber bands

Small dish

Water

Sunny window

LEARNING HOW NATURE GROWS ABOVE AND BELOW THE GROUND

❧ *When Frank Lloyd Wright was a boy, he learned about nature by watching things grow. You can watch a bean plant grow in your window by following these instructions for growing seeds between two pieces of clear glass, which will allow you to see how the plant grows above and below the ground.*

❧ Place one piece of glass on a table top and lay the blotter on top of it. Put the bean seed on the blotter and cover it with the second piece of glass making a sandwich of glass, blotter, seed, and glass. Fasten the sandwich together using rubber bands. Place it in a small dish and fill the dish with water. Draw the bean seed. You may wish to include the blotter, dish, and outline of the plastic in your drawing. When you have finished the drawing, put the dish in a warm, dark place. The seed must remain in the dark until the roots develop. When the bean leaves begin to sprout, place the dish in a window with the bean side facing the sun. Check the water in the dish every day. Add water when the dish is dry. Make a second drawing of the seed when it begins to sprout. Make a third drawing of the bean plant when you notice growth. When the bean has grown into a plant, you may wish to move it outdoors to a pot or plant it in the ground.

❧ Spread your drawings, in the order you drew them, on a table and answer the questions on the next page.

❧ How long did it take the seed to sprout? How long did it take the sprout to grow into a plant? Did the roots develop before the sprout? Did you see a pattern or a shape that repeated itself in the leaves of the plant? Did you see a pattern in the roots?

LEARNING MORE ABOUT THE BASIC GEOMETRIC SHAPES

❧ *Everywhere we look we see shapes. There are shapes we find in nature, and there are shapes of things men and women have made.*

❧ *Shapes are made of lines that enclose space. Some lines are straight and some are curved. Frank Lloyd Wright's boxes of Froebel blocks contained the most basic shapes that can be made from straight and curved lines. These shapes are the circle, the triangle, and the square. They are the basic shapes of geometry.*

❧ There are two kinds of geometry: plane and solid. The Froebel blocks are examples of the shapes of solid geometry. All the shapes in solid geometry have length, width, and thickness. The shape of each Froebel block can also be shown in plane geometry as a flat shape that has only length and width. For example, a square has length and width. It is a flat shape from plane geometry. A cube is a solid square. Because it has length, width, and thickness, it is a shape from solid geometry. In the same way, a circle is a flat shape from plane geometry, and a sphere is the same shape in solid geometry. A triangle is a flat shape from plane geometry, and a pyramid is the same shape in solid geometry.

❧ Frank Lloyd Wright used the shapes of plane geometry to design decorations and to draw the plans for his buildings. He used the shapes of solid geometry to make his buildings.

❧ The basic shapes of solid geometry are drawn with shading, which allows us to see that each shape has length, width, and thickness. The basic shapes of plane geometry are drawn with lines only.

❧ A circle is a space closed by a curved line that is always the same distance from the center of the circle. The two other basic geometric shapes, the triangle and the square, are all called polygons in plane geometry. Polygons are many-sided shapes with closed sides made from straight lines. All polygons have at least three sides. The places where two sides of a polygon meet are called angles. Regular polygons have all sides and angles equal.

❧ When we add thickness to the shape of a circle we call it a sphere. When we add thickness to the shapes of the regular polygons we call them regular polyhedrons. Spheres and polyhedrons are shapes in solid geometry.

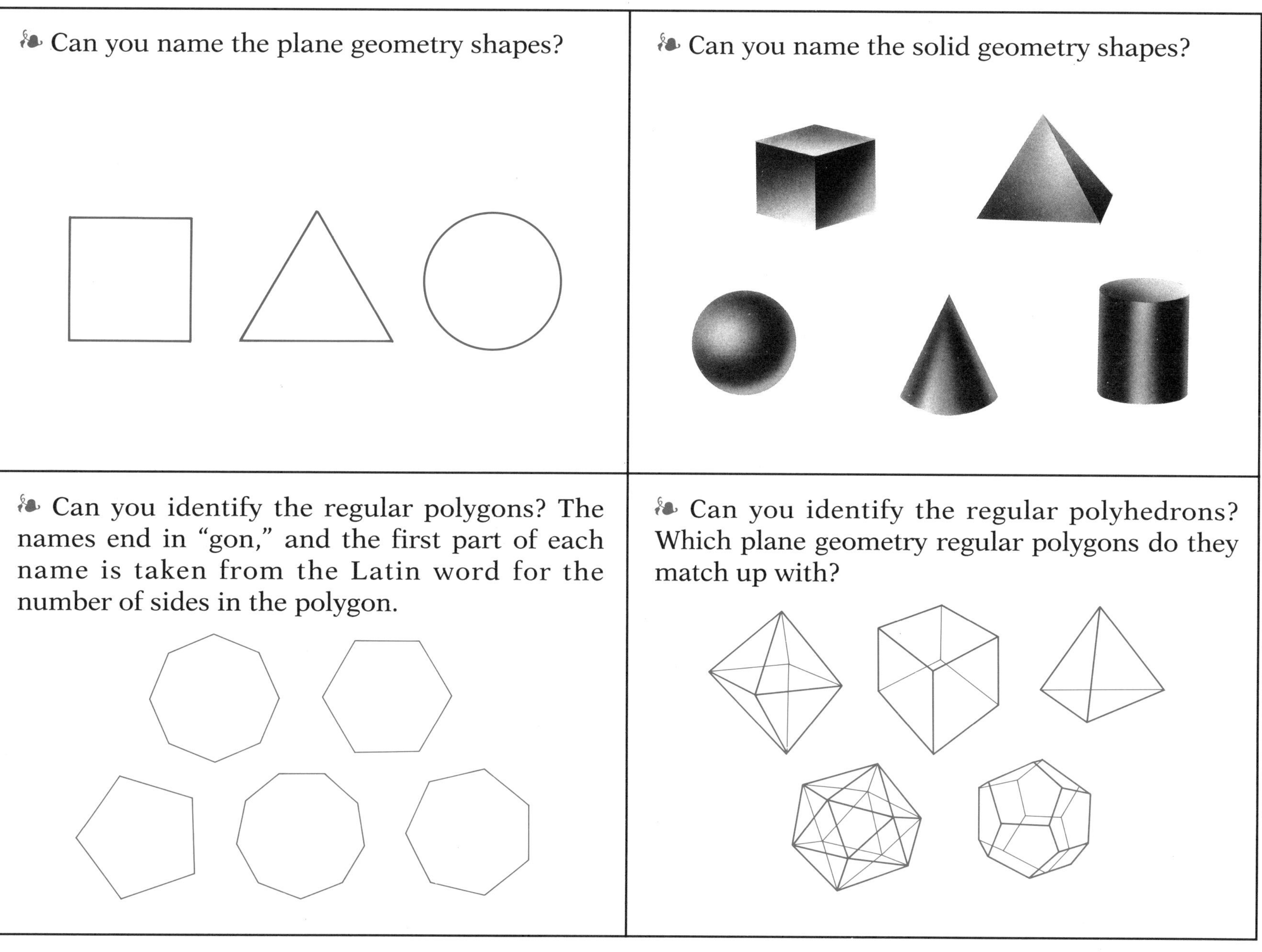
Can you name the plane geometry shapes?
Can you name the solid geometry shapes?
Can you identify the regular polygons? The names end in "gon," and the first part of each name is taken from the Latin word for the number of sides in the polygon.
Can you identify the regular polyhedrons? Which plane geometry regular polygons do they match up with?

FINDING THE HIDDEN SHAPES WITHIN THE OBJECTS

❧ Frank Lloyd Wright believed that everything is made from basic geometric shapes. The shapes can be hidden within the object, but they are there just the same.

❧ The shapes of the Froebel blocks are hidden in the picture. Some are the shapes of solid geometry, and some are the shapes of plane geometry. How many can you find?

DISCOVERING PATTERNS MADE WITH SHAPES

While Frank Lloyd Wright was playing with his Froebel blocks he may have noticed that his mother and sisters were using the same geometric shapes for needlework projects. In the 1870s, women often spent their free time making cross-stitch samplers. The imaginative shapes of fruits, flowers, birds, animals, trees, houses, and letters were all created from groups of tiny square stitches. The square cross-stitch is the hidden basic geometric shape used to make the simple everyday objects on samplers.

The patchwork quilt was another kind of needlework that used the basic shapes of plane geometry: the circle, the triangle, and the square. When Frank Lloyd Wright was a boy, patchwork quilts were needed to keep people warm during cold winters. An old quilt pattern, nicknamed the Ohio Star, shows how a star shape can be made from squares and triangles. Another pattern, called the Maple Leaf, shows a maple leaf simplified to the basic geometric shapes.

Guess the name of the object shown in each of the three well-known quilt patterns.

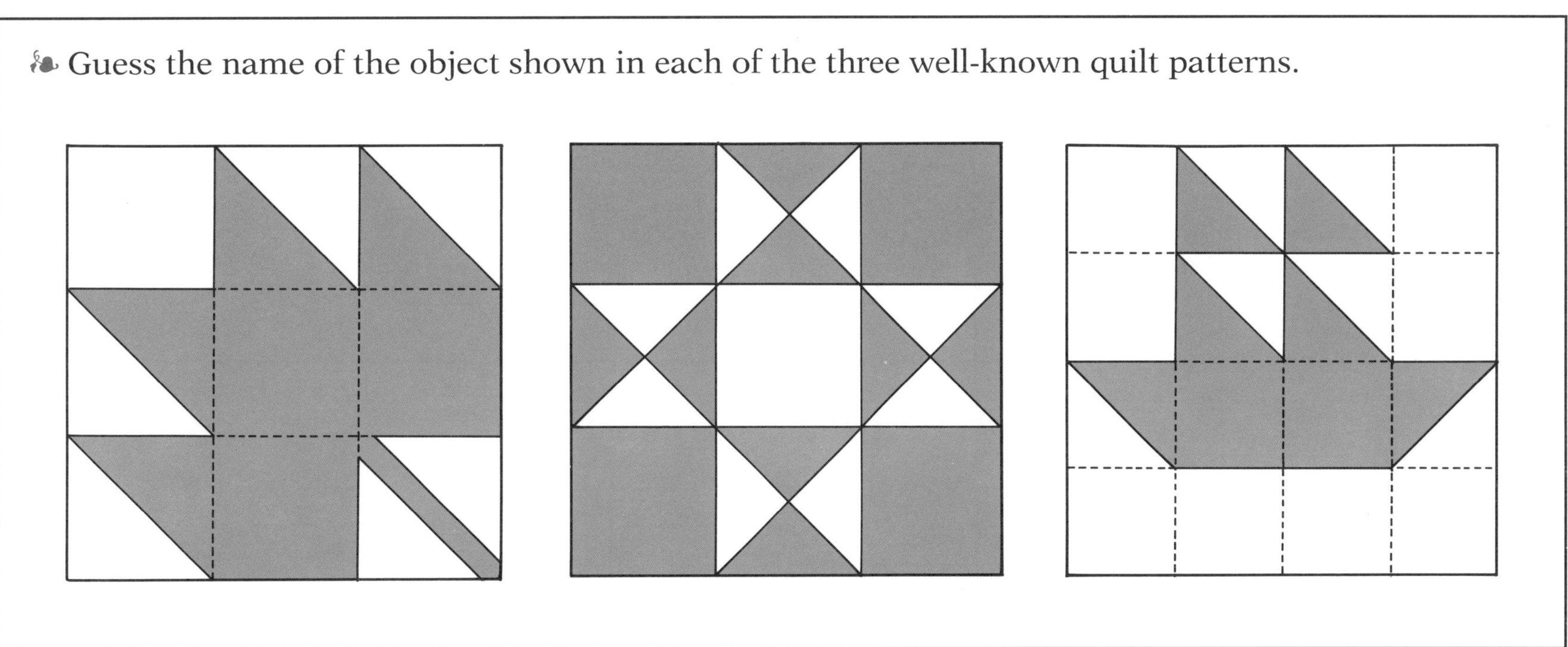

❧ Frank Lloyd Wright's design for the Coonley children's playhouse windows is shown below. Windows made from patterns of colored and clear glass are called stained glass windows. They are made from many pieces of glass held together with strips of lead. The strips of lead are shown as heavy black lines in the drawing.

❧ The Coonley playhouse windows are made from red, blue, green, black, and clear glass. The shapes are carefully arranged on a grid of horizontal and vertical lines. One of the basic geometric shapes is missing from the design. Which one is it? The shapes work together to make a familiar object that is somewhat hidden in the window. What is it?

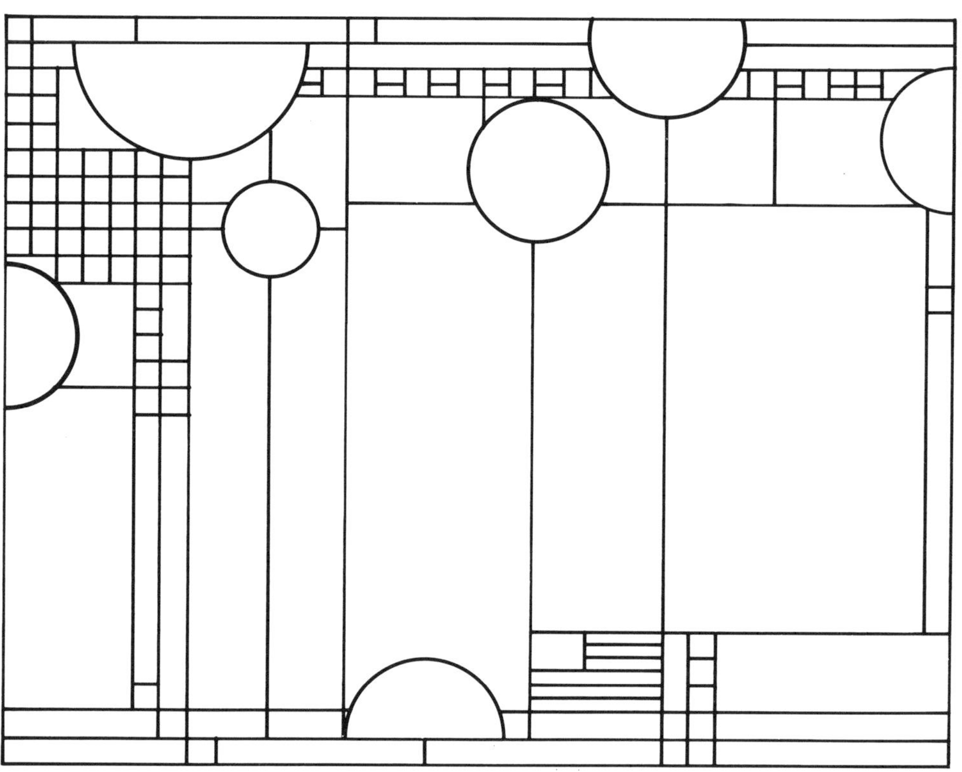

❧ It is easy to cut shapes for the colored places in the window from paper and move them around. Remember to leave some areas white to represent clear glass. Because you are making a design for a stained glass window, you should arrange your final design on a grid of horizontal and vertical lines. Use the ruler to draw the lines in pencil on your paper. Space them one inch apart in each direction. When you have found a design that pleases you, paste the shapes in place. Draw in the lines with a black marker connecting the shapes. The black lines represent the lead used to hold the glass in place.

❧ If you know an adult who can sew, you may ask for help in turning your stained glass window design into a small quilt. Since it is easier to sew pieces with straight edges together, it is best to make a quilt design that uses only straight lines.

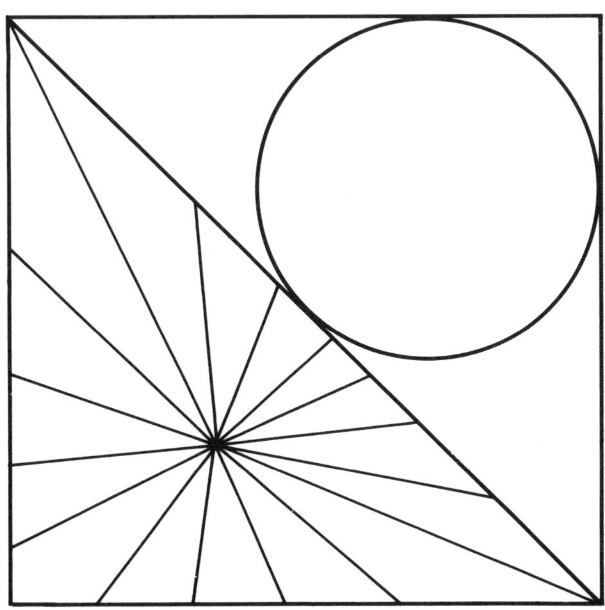

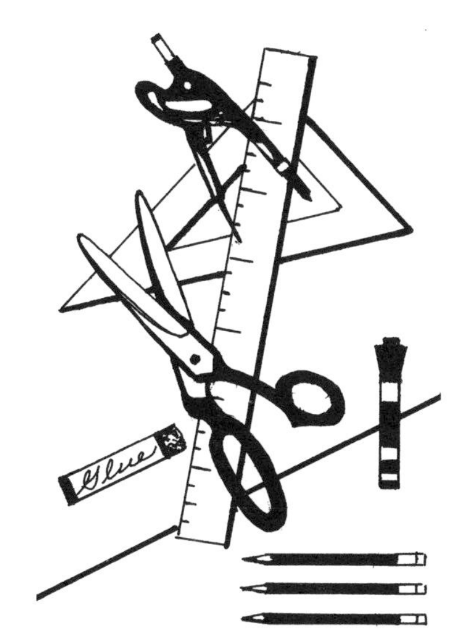

Materials

Several sheets of colored origami or construction paper

Large sheet of white construction paper

Scissors

Glue stick

Compass

Ruler and triangle

Pencils

Black marker

Materials
Ruler
Compass
Triangle (optional)
Scissors
Heavy paper or cardboard
Pencils

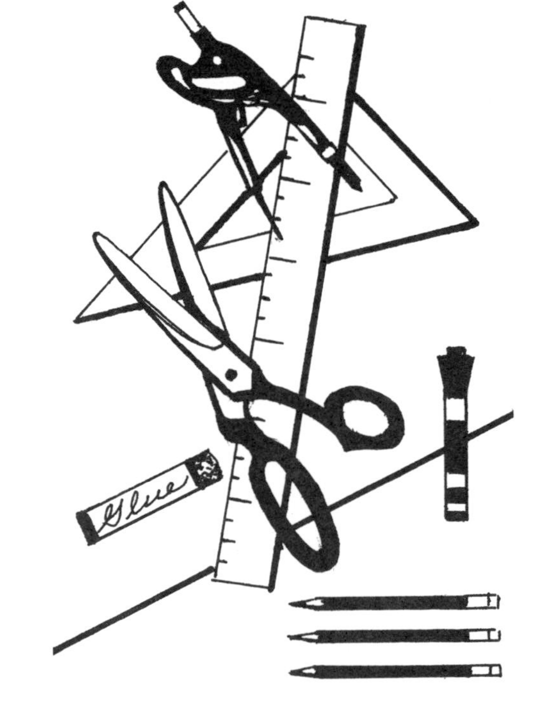

LEARNING ABOUT SYMMETRY

❧ *Shapes that are exactly the same on either side of a line have symmetry and may be called symmetric shapes. In nature, the wings of a butterfly are the same shape on either side of the butterfly's body. Therefore, a butterfly's wings are symmetric. There are many more examples of symmetry found in nature. Many leaves are symmetric. In fact, the human face and body have symmetry. If a line is drawn through the nose down the center of a human face, there will be one eye, one eyebrow, one cheek, and one ear on each side of the line.*

❧ If there is symmetry in nature, then there must also be symmetry in basic geometric shapes. A line drawn from the top of a triangle straight to the bottom will divide the triangle into two smaller, equal symmetric triangles. A line drawn anywhere through the center of a circle will divide it into two symmetric half-circles. A line drawn through the center of a square will divide it into two rectangles.

❧ Draw your own symmetric design using the basic shapes of plane geometry. This will be easier if you first draw the shapes on a piece of heavy paper or cardboard and cut them out. Then you can lay the cutout shapes over the printed graph paper and trace around them. Before you begin, draw a heavy black line down the center of the graph paper. When you are finished, the shapes on either side of the heavy center line must match exactly.

❧ Frank Lloyd Wright used symmetry when he drew the design for the skylight in his dining room.

❧ How many examples of symmetry can you find in the smaller parts of Frank Lloyd Wright's design? How many examples of symmetry are in the complete design? How many shapes found in nature can you recognize?

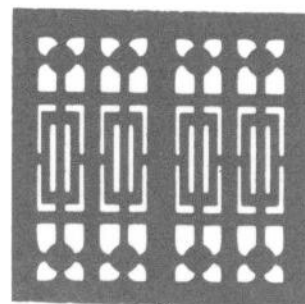

COMPARING THE DESIGN OF HOUSES

❧ *Before Frank Lloyd Wright drew the plans for his house in Oak Park, he spent a long time thinking about all of the things he did not like about Victorian houses. On the next page you can see a photograph of Frank Lloyd Wright's house and one of a Victorian house. Victorian houses are sometimes nicknamed "gingerbread houses" because they have as many decorations as gaily decorated gingerbread cookies.*

❧ When architectural historians study houses they look at all of the things that are the same in houses that were built at about the same time. When they find a group of houses with a fairly long list of similarities, a name, such as Victorian or shingle, is chosen for the houses in the group. These names are called architectural styles. Many houses have bits and pieces of different architectural styles, so these names give us only an idea of the main style of a house.

❧ The style name of the Victorian house in our picture is "Queen Anne." This name was chosen because many houses that looked like this were built during the reign of England's Queen Anne. Frank Lloyd Wright's house is a shingle-style house. This name was chosen because the houses in this group are usually completely covered with wooden shingles.

❧ Have you ever wanted to know more about the houses in your neighborhood? A picture and the names of some of the main styles of American houses are shown on the following pages with a few characteristics of each style. Try matching the houses in your block to these architectural styles.

❧ Can you see the basic geometric shapes hidden in Frank Lloyd Wright's house? What are they? Would you have an easy time building this house with a set of Froebel blocks? How many blocks would you need to build the basic shape of the house? Can you see the basic geometric shapes hidden in the Victorian house? Could you build it with Froebel blocks? How many blocks would you need to build the Victorian house?

Colonial

English

Craftsman

Prairie

Spanish

Bungalow

Ranch

Modern

INTERVIEWING A LONG-TIME RESIDENT OF YOUR NEIGHBORHOOD

❧ *Do you have any neighbors who have been living on your block for more than twenty-five years? These people can tell you interesting things about the way things used to be. This project suggests you make an appointment with one of the neighborhood long-timers and ask questions about the history of your neighborhood. If your neighborhood is new, ask your parents to help you find an older neighborhood. Write about the interview on a notepad, or record it with a tape recorder.*

❧ Select a neighbor who has lived on your block for at least twenty-five years. Your parents can tell you which neighbors will enjoy being interviewed. Telephone them to set an interview time or leave a note telling them about your project and asking them to call you.

❧ Write the neighbor's name and address on a notepad. If you have a tape recorder, be sure it is working properly. Do both of these things before you go to the interview. Be sure to arrive on time.

❧ Ask the following questions, adding questions of your own as you think of them:

Where and when were you born?

How long have you lived in this neighborhood?

How long have you lived in this house?

What did it look like when you moved in?

What changes has your family made to the house? Why?

What changes have you noticed in this neighborhood?

Which neighbor has lived here the longest?

How have houses changed in the last twenty-five years?

Has the way families use houses changed in the last twenty-five years?

How has your kitchen changed? Your bathroom? Your living room?

❧ When you have finished your interview, play the tape for your family and talk about the changes in the neighborhood.

SEARCHING FOR CLUES TO THE HISTORY OF OLD HOUSES

❧ *Most historic houses that have been designed by famous architects like Frank Lloyd Wright and are now open for the public to tour have been "restored." This means that the buildings have been returned to the way they looked in the past. This is not always the way they looked the year when the house was new. It can be, as in the case of President Harry Truman's house in Independence, Missouri, the way the house was when President Truman and his wife Bess last lived in it in the late fifties, even though the Victorian house was originally built in the late 1800s.*

❧ People who restore houses must first decide on the what year they wish to return the house. In the case of the families living in old homes, the decision is made by the family. In the case of houses that are museums, this decision is made by the people running the museum.

❧ Most old houses have changed in one way or another over time. They may have belonged to several different families who have had different needs and tastes in home decoration. Many of them have been remodeled. Rooms have been added or taken away to make way for different sized families. Kitchens and bathrooms have changed to make room for new appliances and different family lifestyles.

❧ When a house is restored as a museum, careful studies are made of the way the house used to look. Restoration research is usually done by a specialist or professional architect, but it can also be done by you. If you live in an old house or know

Materials

Notepad

Pencils

Strong flashlight

Screwdriver

someone who does, you can be a detective and search for clues to the past history of the house.

❧ Be sure you have the permission and assistance of an adult who lives in the house before you begin your search. Don't remove anything from the walls without adult permission and assistance. If a suitable old house is not easy for you to find, ask your parents to take you to a local historical house that is open for tours. A docent will usually explain the discovery of clues and the story of the restoration during the tour.

❧ Begin by talking to the owner of the house. Write down your information on the notepad. Ask if the owner has the building plans. Check at the local building department (usually found in the city hall) to see if permits for additions to the house were issued. Old photographs and conversations with people who used to live in the house can provide valuable clues to what the house looked like long ago.

❧ Old toilets are usually marked with the date they were made.

❧ Windows can help identify the date a house was built and show where changes have been made to a house. It is common for colonial-style houses to have windows made from many separate panes of glass that are all the same size. Each individual pane of glass is called a "light," and the windows are called six-light or eight-light windows. The date a colonial house was built can be determined by the number of window lights.

❧ Different window styles help identify places where a house has been changed. It is easy to spot household remodeling that was done after 1945 because it was popular to use louver windows and sliding glass doors at that time.

❧ Pieces of old wallpaper or paint colors may be hidden under light switch plates and mounted wall fixtures. Sometimes they can be found in closets, under mirrors, or behind built-in drawers and inside window seats. These clues will tell you what color the walls were originally.

❧ Search the basement or attic with a flashlight. Basements usually have more clues than attics. Look for old pipes or wires that were left behind when the house was remodeled. They can show you where a kitchen sink was located originally or where walls have been moved. Look for the foundation of a chimney that may have been removed from the top floors of the house. Look for notes with dates that have been written on the walls by workmen.

❧ When you have finished your search, write a brief history of the house and the changes that have been made to it. Be sure to include the date the house was built and the date of your search.

READING ARCHITECTURAL PLANS TO SOLVE A MAZE

When Frank Lloyd Wright dreamed about building a house over the waterfall on Bear Run, he wrote the Kaufmanns a long letter describing his ideas. However, when the Kaufmanns came to visit him at Taliesin, he needed more than words to describe his ideas. He needed drawings to help them see what the house would look like.

To help us understand how Frank Lloyd Wright made drawings to show his clients, we can look at a drawing on page 85 taken from the instruction book that came with Frank Lloyd Wright's set of Froebel blocks.

The other drawings—top view and front and side elevations—are nicknamed "the plans" and serve as the main drawings all architects must prepare when they design a house. "The plans" are shown to clients to help them understand what a house will look like, and they are shown to building contractors so they will know exactly how to build the house.

The top view is like a map of the house that tells us where everything is. Architects use two parallel lines to show where the walls are. If the space between the lines is colored in, the walls extend vertically from the floor to the ceiling. If the space between the lines is open, the walls are "free-standing" walls, such as garden walls.

It is hard for first time visitors to the Robie House to find the front door. Perhaps the house was designed this way because Mr. Robie required extra privacy; perhaps Frank Lloyd Wright wanted visitors to have the impression that they were visiting a ship. Picture a large ship in your mind. Is there a front door in the picture?

Since the Robie House is built on a corner lot, it has two sides facing the street. An ordinary house would have the front door in the center of the longest street side. Most ordinary front doors would have a porch or some kind of decoration around them making it very obvious to everyone that this is the correct place to enter the house.

The tiny footprints on the first floor plan of the Robie House, on page 84, show the path a visitor has to take to find the front door if they choose to enter the house from the longest street side. The only opening to the sidewalk on this side of the house is through the driveway. Pretend you are visiting the Robie House for the first time and decide to enter through the driveway. Once inside the garden walls, your long trip around the house will take you past the following items.

❧ How many steps? How many doors (not counting the front door)? How many windows? How many trees and shrubs?

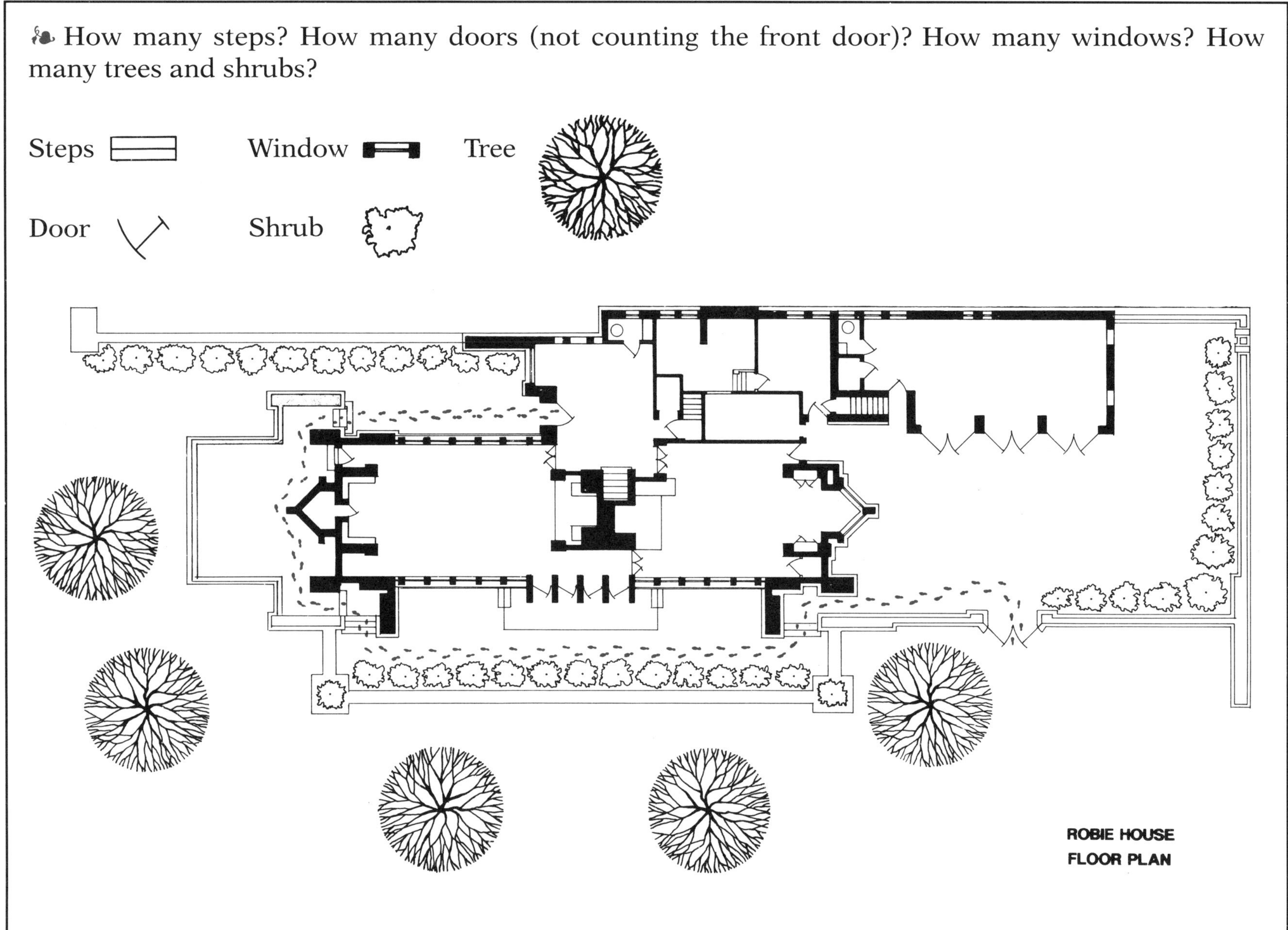

❧ In this drawing of a little house it is easy to see the basic geometric shapes hidden in the outer shape of the house.

❧ If the roof and ceiling were taken off of the little house and we were flying in a helicopter looking down on it, the house would look like this. It is called a "floor plan."

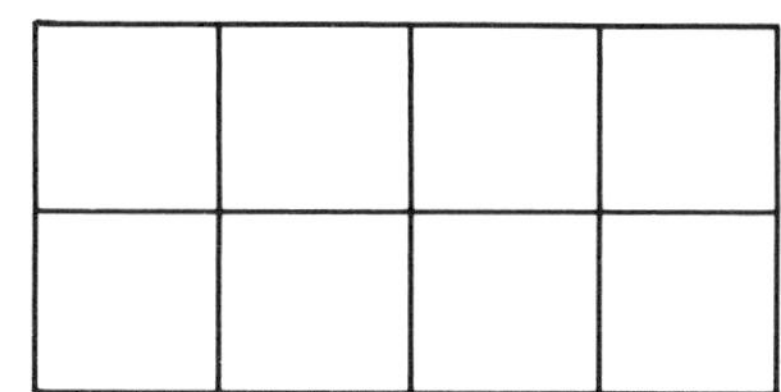

❧ If we were standing on the front side of the little house and looking straight at it, we would see this. It is called a "front elevation."

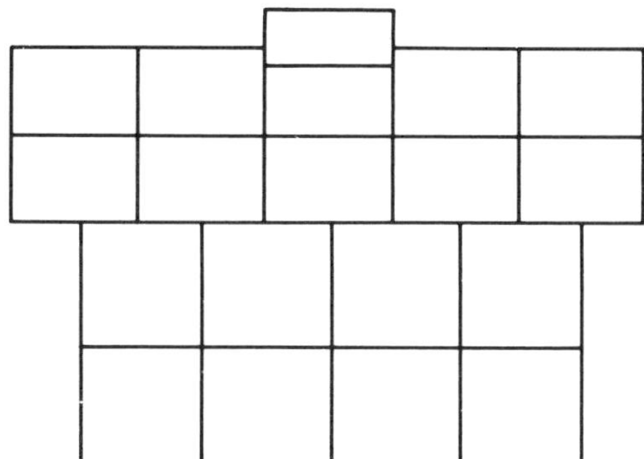

❧ If we were standing on the long side of the little house and looking straight at it, we would see this. It is called a "side elevation."

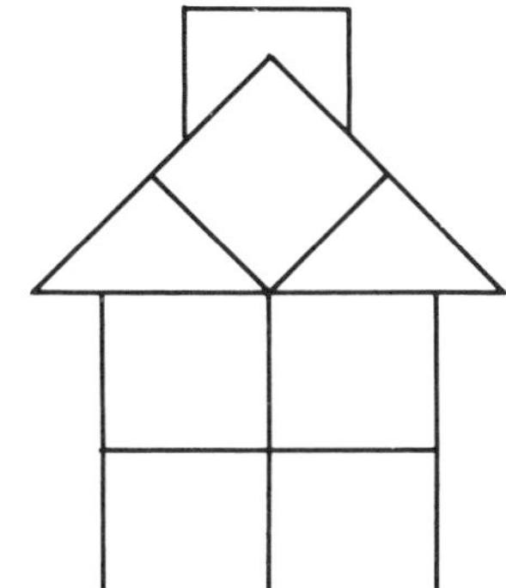

DRAWING REALISTIC AND ABSTRACT FLOWERS

❧ *The flowers Frank Lloyd Wright used to decorate the Hollyhock House were simplified to the basic shapes of the Froebel blocks. Some of the flowers that decorate the house are drawn using plane geometry, and some use shapes from solid geometry.*

❧ There is not much difference between the photograph on the left and the first drawing on the next page, because both the photograph and drawing are realistic pictures that show us how hollyhocks look when they have length, width, and thickness. We see the flowers as shapes in solid geometry.

❧ In the second drawing on the next page, the flower shapes have only length and width. They are shapes in plane geometry.

❧ In the last drawing, the flower has been drawn using only flat geometric shapes. The process of simplifying shapes from the very realistic, shaded shapes of solid geometry to the flat, one-color shapes of plane geometry is called abstraction.

❧ Frank Lloyd Wright simplified or abstracted the realistic shapes of a real hollyhock flower to the flat geometric shapes of the flowers he used to decorate the Hollyhock House. We do not know how many drawings he made before he drew the final patterns for the abstract hollyhocks, but, if we work with a photograph and several drawings, we can begin to see the process he used.

❧ On a clean sheet of paper, draw the tulip flower using the basic geometric shapes in the same way Frank Lloyd Wright drew the hollyhock flower.

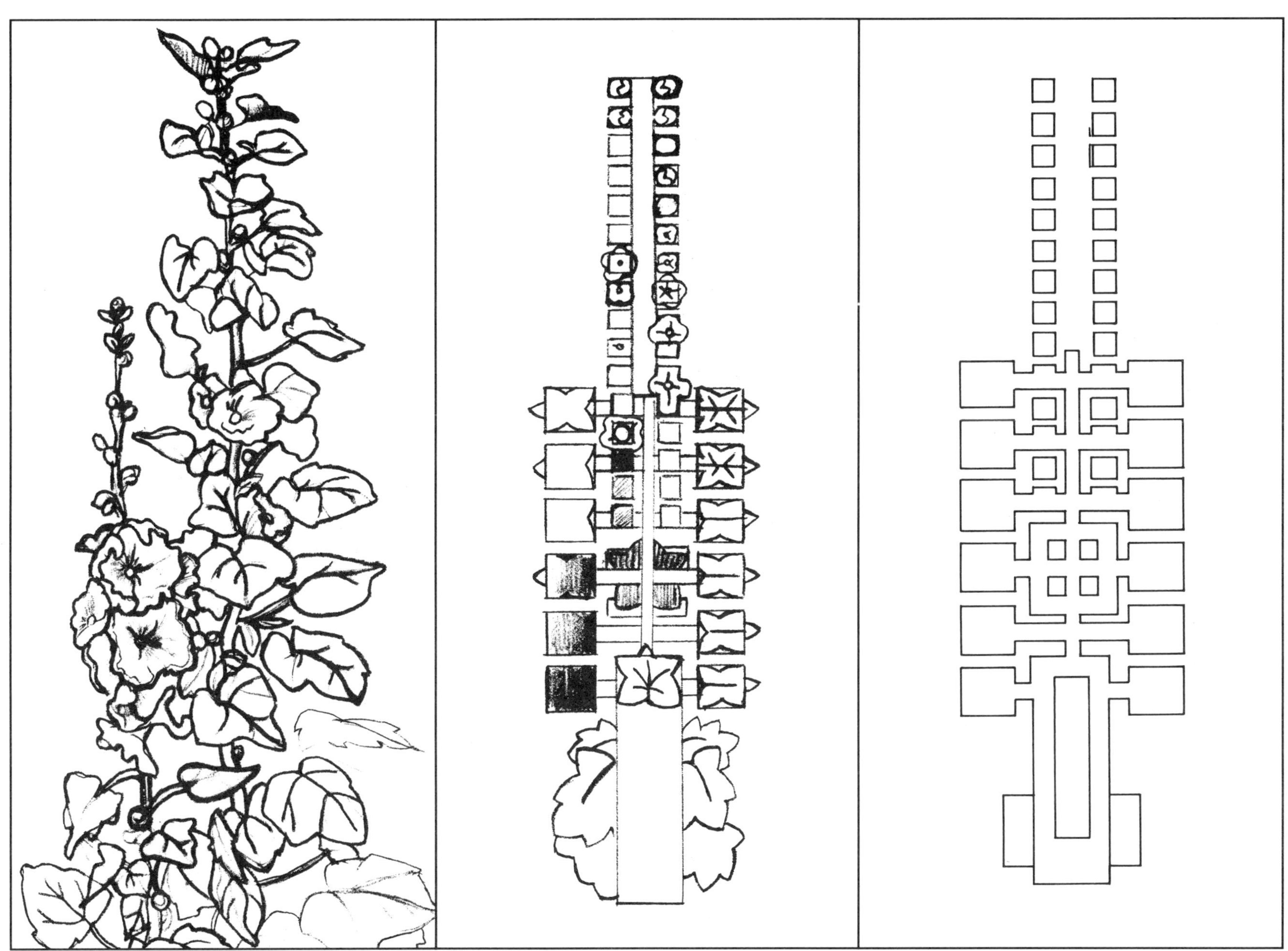

Materials

Three pieces origami paper, approximately 4½ by 4½ inches

Clean worktable

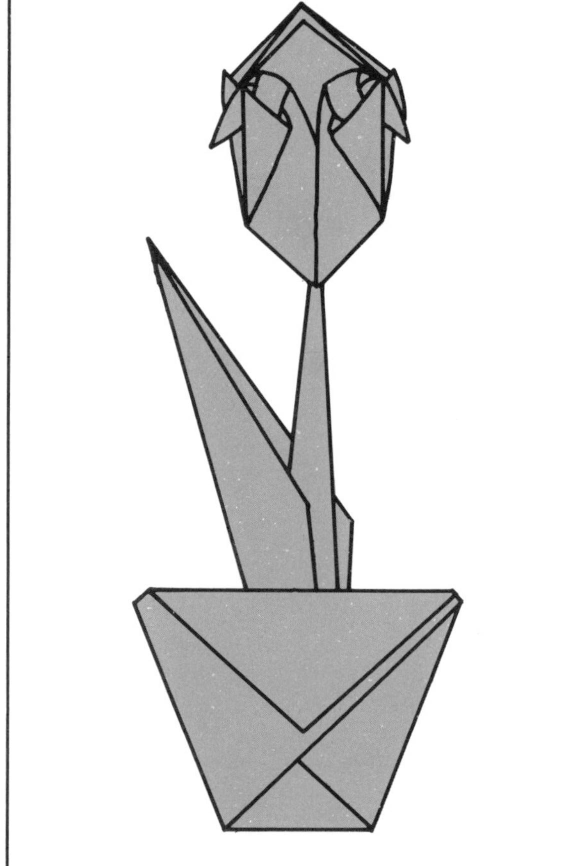

MAKING A PAPER FLOWER FROM BASIC GEOMETRIC SHAPES

Another way to learn to see the hidden shapes within an object is to fold simple shapes with paper. In Japan, ways of making birds, flowers, and animals from folded paper were passed from generation to generation. This playful paper craft is called origami. Origami objects are made from small squares of paper without gluing, cutting, or stapling. Since the shape of all origami folds are the basic geometric shapes of the triangle, square, and rectangle, origami is another way for you to learn to see the hidden shapes within an object. Directions follow for three simple origami projects: a flower pot, a stem and leaf, and a tulip flower.

For these projects you will need a package of multicolored origami paper. Origami paper is sold in arts and crafts shops, stationery and toy stores, and oriental gift shops. If you cannot find this paper, have one of your parents help you cut plain white squares from any medium-weight paper. If you are cutting your own squares, they must be carefully measured and cut into perfect squares.

FLOWER POT ❧ Step 1

Begin working with the white side of the paper up. Fold the paper in half along one of the diagonals.

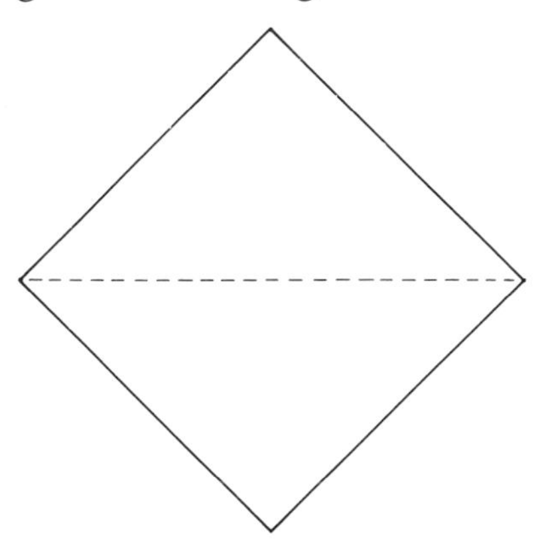

❧ Step 2

Fold point **A** to meet point **B** and crease along the fold.

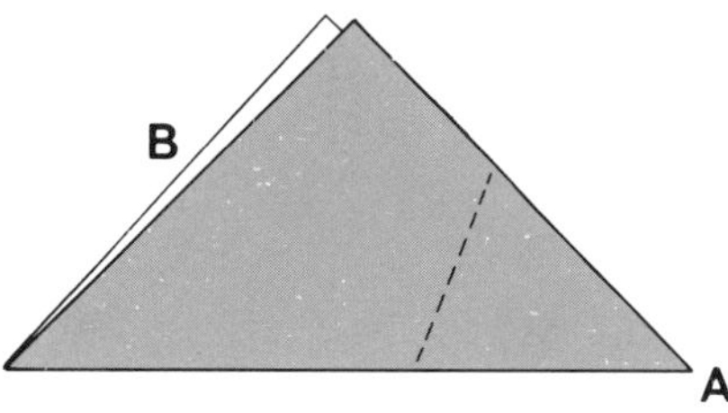

❧ Step 3

Fold point **C** to meet point **D** and crease along the fold.

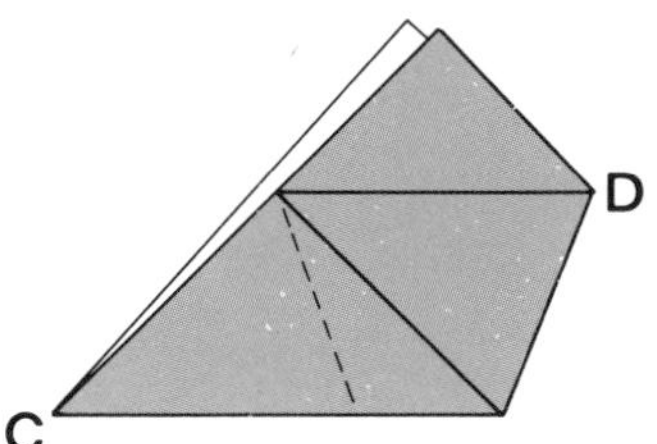

❧ Step 4

There are two flaps of paper at the top of the flower pot. Fold one flap to the outside and crease along the fold.

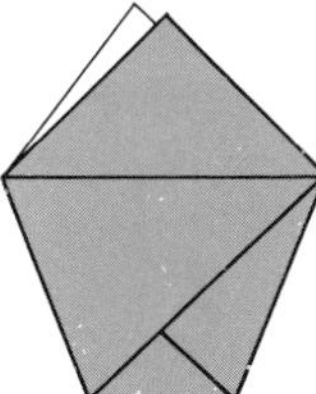

❧ Step 5

Turn the paper over and fold the second flap of paper to the outside. Crease along the fold.

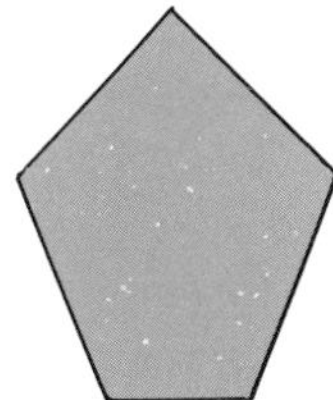

❧ Step 6

You should be holding a small cup shape with an opening in the top. The drawings show the front and back sides of the flower pot.

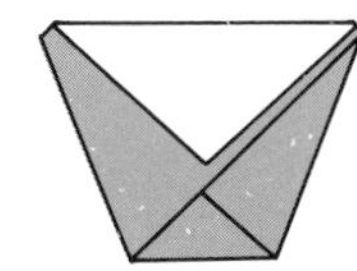

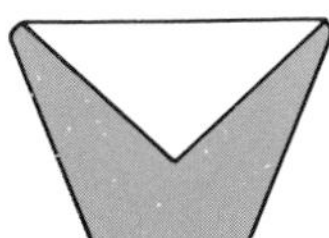

STEM AND LEAF ❧ Step 1

Beginning with the white side of the paper up, fold and crease it along the diagonal. Open the paper and lay it flat on the table, white side up.

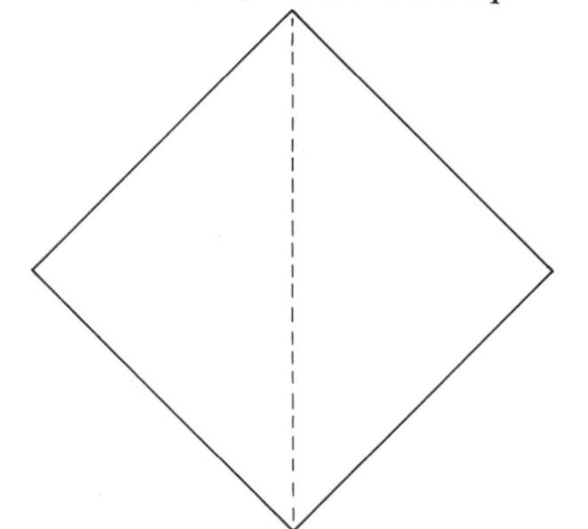

❧ Step 2

Fold the bottom two outside edges to the line made by the fold in the center of the paper, lining the outside edges up with the center line. Crease along the two new folds.

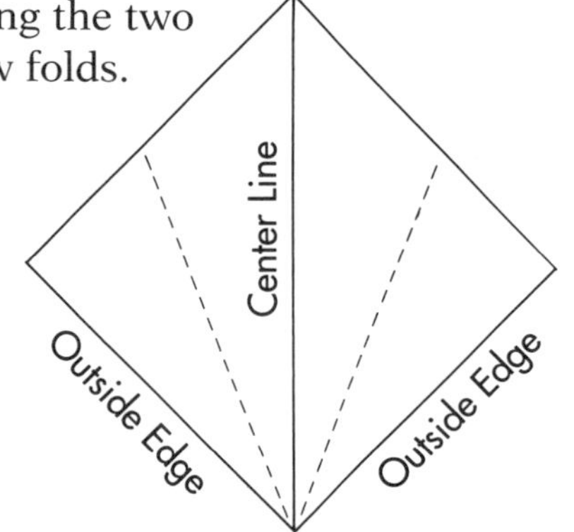

❧ Step 3

Without turning the paper, fold the upper two outside edges to the center, lining the outside edges up with the center line. Crease along the new folds.

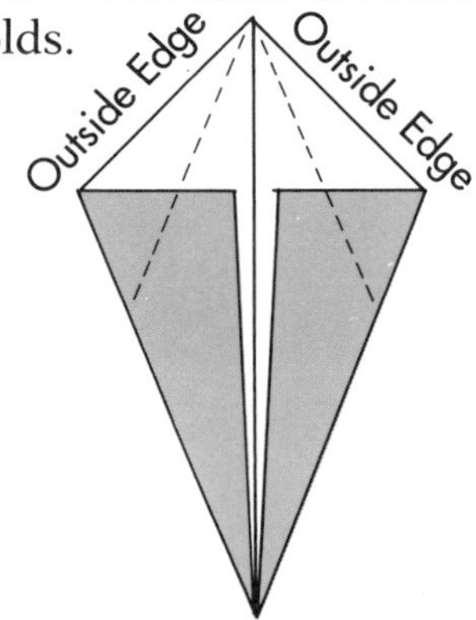

❧ Step 4

Without turning the paper, fold the outside edges to the center, lining the bottom two outside edges up with the center line. Crease along the new fold.

❧ Step 5

Without turning the paper, fold in half (from bottom to top) matching point **A** up with point **B**. Crease along the new fold.

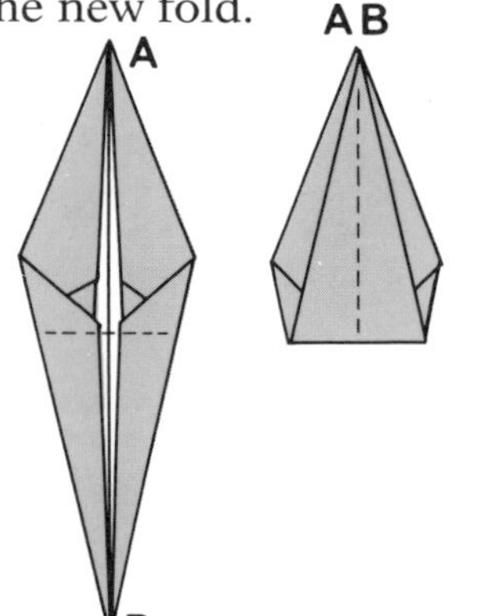

❧ Step 6

Without turning the paper, fold in half (from side to side) matching the outside edges. Crease, and keep the paper folded. Hold firmly at the bottom and pull the points at the top away from each other.

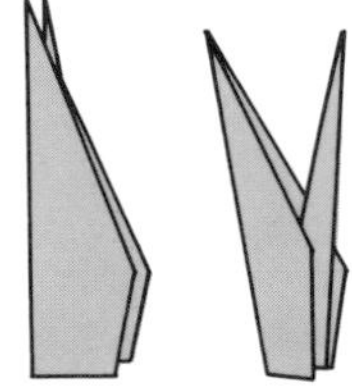

TULIP FLOWER ❧ Step 1

Beginning with the white side of the paper up, fold and crease it along both diagonals. Open the paper and lay it flat on the table, white side up.

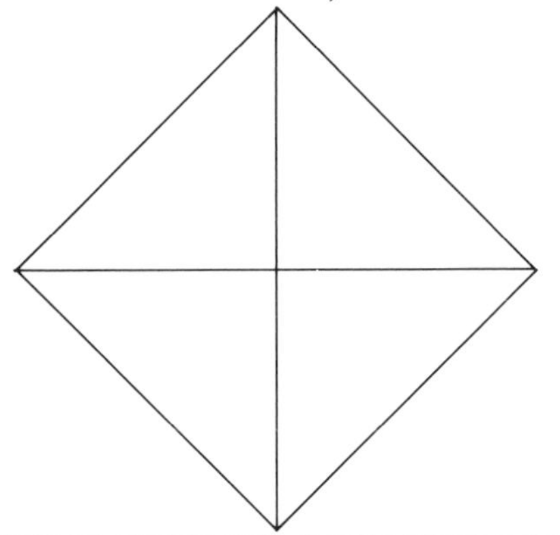

❧ Step 2

Fold the four corner points in to the center. Crease along the four folds.

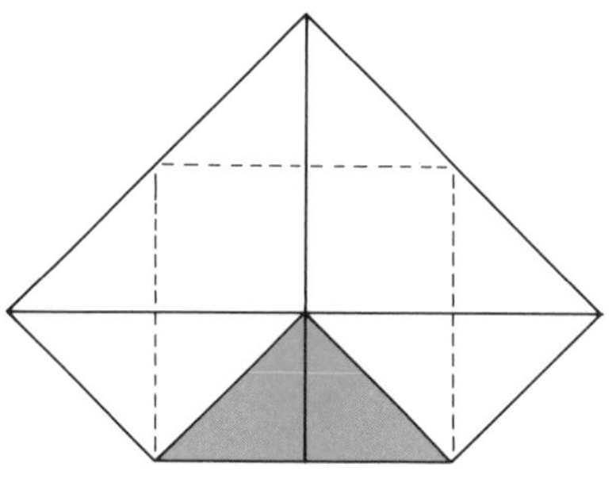

❧ Step 3

You now have a smaller square of paper, colored on both sides. One side is a solid piece of paper; the other has four loose flaps. Fold in half and crease. The loose flaps should be popping up on the outside.

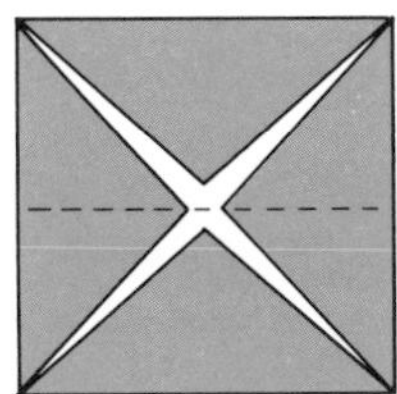

❧ Step 4

Fold point **A** in to the solid side of the paper. In origami this is called a "reverse fold" because the paper is folded from the outside to the inside. Do not wrap to the front or back of the paper.

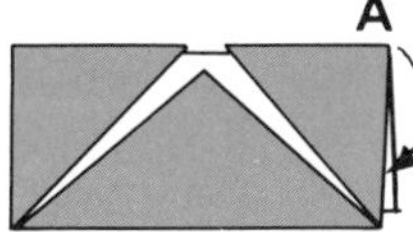

❧ Step 5

"Reverse fold" **B** to the solid side of the paper.

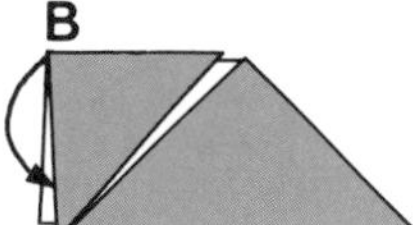

❧ Step 6

The paper now has triangles on the top and bottom. Place it on the table and work only with the triangle that is on top. Fold points **E** and **D** to meet point **C** at the top of the triangle. Crease.

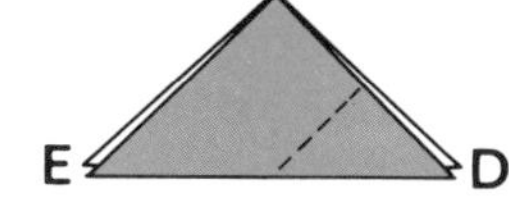

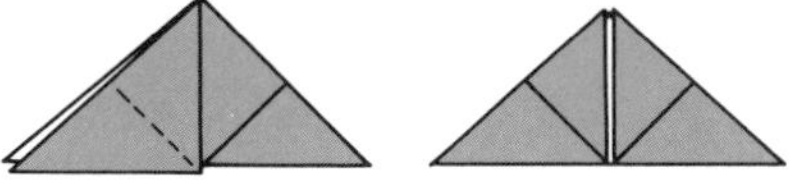

Step 7

Turn the paper over and make the same folds as in Step 5. Crease along the new folds. The paper is now a many-layered square.

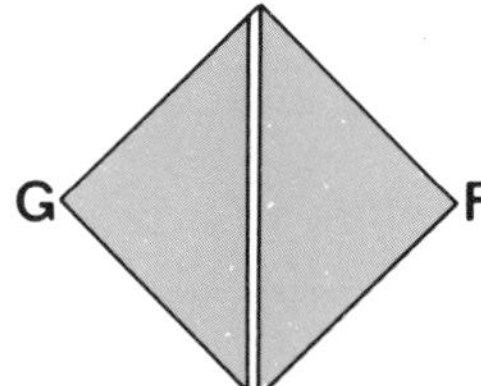

Step 8

Working with the flaps in the top side of the paper, fold points **F** and **G** to the center. Crease along the new folds.

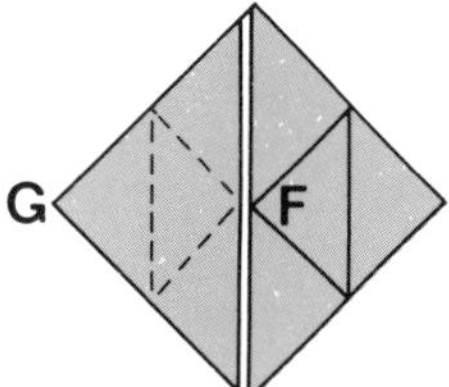

Step 9

Turn the paper over and repeat Step 7 with the flaps on the other side. The paper should now have this shape on both sides.

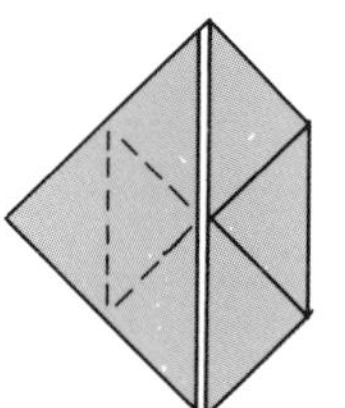

Step 10

There are many layers of triangles at the top and bottom. Gently pull the paper apart at the top to find two loose triangles on each side. Each triangle should be tucked into the paper pocket just below and creased lightly.

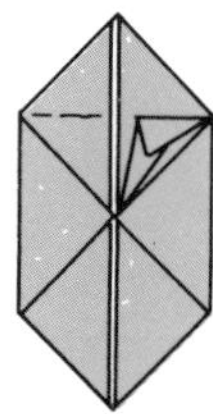

Step 11

Hold the paper at the bottom and separate the layers of paper at the top. You will see a pattern of white triangles at the top. Gently separate them and the flower will open up.

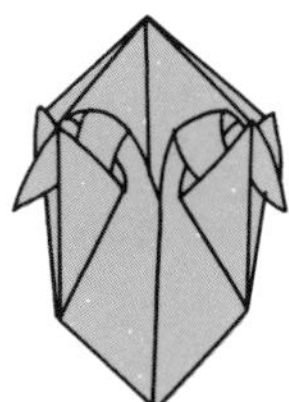

ASSEMBLING THE POT, STEM AND LEAF, AND TULIP FLOWER

Gently push the tip of the stem up into the tiny hole in the bottom of the flower and slide the bottom of the stem into the pot.

How many different geometric shapes did you see while you folded the pot? the stem? the flower?

EXPERIMENTING WITH COLORS

Frank Lloyd Wright used the rainbow of colors he found in nature to make his houses feel pleasant and comfortable for the people who lived in them. In the fifties, he chose a group of his favorite colors and had them printed so that other people could use them in their houses. He called the colors the Taliesin Palette. Most of these colors were named after nature. The Taliesin Palette had Spring Green, Sun Tan, Raspberry, Shell Pink Midnight, Cloud White, Bluebird, Oak Bark, Sky Blue, Autumn Green, and Cornfield Tan. These colors reminded Frank Lloyd Wright of the soft and beautiful way colors blend together in nature.

The Japanese make beautiful colored designs on paper by folding and tying paper and then dying it. Paper dying shows how the primary colors—red, yellow, and blue—blend together to form orange, green, and violet. The softness of the colors blending together on the paper reminds us of the way colors blend together in nature.

You can order powdered food colors from the Maid of Scandinavia catalog, 3244 Raleigh Avenue, Minneapolis, Minnesota 55416. They are more brilliant than the liquid kind. Sumi-E paper can be purchased at art supply stores on a continuous roll or in pads.

Materials

Several medium-sized bowls

Clean worktable protected with newspapers or a plastic cover

Red, blue, and yellow food coloring

White vinegar

Water

1⅛-by-24-inch pad Sumi-E Painting-Sketch paper or 1 pad newsprint

Paper

Rubber band

Marbles

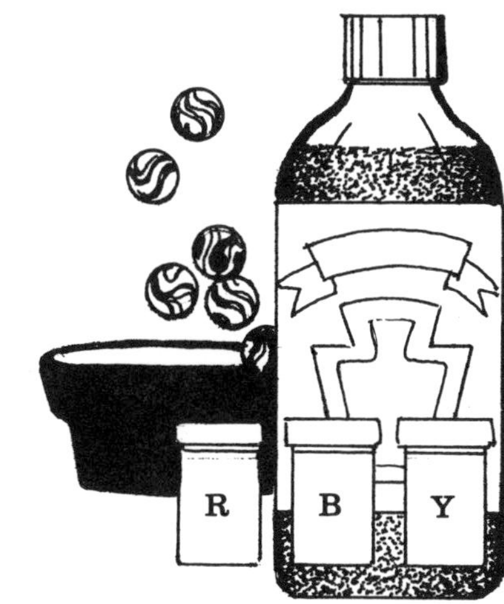

❧ Place the mixing bowls on the table. Add 2 tablespoons of liquid or 1 teaspoon powdered food coloring to each bowl. Add 1 tablespoon of white vinegar and ¼ cup water to each bowl. Stir to mix the colors.

❧ Remove one sheet from the pad of paper. Handle the paper gently or it will tear. Fold it into an accordion shape. Fold the accordion shape in half and quickly dip and remove the center part from the red dye. Unfold the paper and dip one end in the blue dye and one end in the yellow dye. Be careful not to hold the paper in the dye too long. It will soak up too much liquid and tear.

❧ The red and blue dyes mixed together to make violet, and the red and yellow mixed together to make orange. If you dye the middle of the second paper accordion yellow, what colors will you get on the ends?

❧ Fold a second sheet of paper in half twice, use it to cover a marble, and fasten it with a rubber band. Dip the entire thing in the red dye and then dip just the tip of the marble in the blue dye.

❧ Fold a third piece of paper in half over and over until it is a small packet. Dip each corner of the small square in a different colored dye. Set the paper aside to dry slightly for about 15 minutes so that it will not tear when you try to unfold it.

❧ Working over the table, remove the rubber band. Slowly and carefully unfold each piece of paper and spread it out to dry. You will see that each one has a different pattern made by the dyes. Set the paper aside to dry slightly for about 15 minutes so that it will not tear when you try to unfold it.

❧ Continue to experiment with folding and color blending. The drawings below show some other tying and folding ideas. When you are finished, save your color-blending experiments. They will make beautiful wrapping paper.

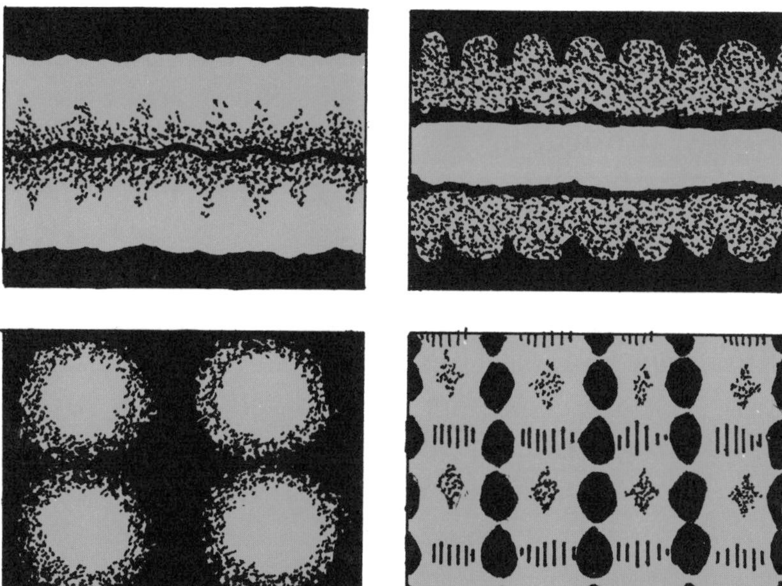

BUILDING A CANTILEVER AND A MODEL OF FALLINGWATER WITH GRAHAM CRACKERS

❧ *Fallingwater is probably Frank Lloyd Wright's most famous house. Fallingwater's closeness to nature and its position right over a waterfall make the house unforgettable, but, when we look at a picture of Fallingwater, the thing we notice first are the cantilevers. The cantilevers make the house look like a tree growing over a waterfall. Tree branches are cantilevers made by nature. The branch is attached or supported at one end only—at the trunk. A diving board is another example of a cantilever—an object that extends out into space and is supported at only one end.*

❧ You can build a cantilever with objects you find around your house. Bricks or blocks will work very well. You will need 6 to 8 rectangular blocks of the same size. Make a base of three blocks and place a fourth block on top of them at a right angle. This block will fall off unless you support it at one end with one or two more blocks. When block number four is held in place without the help of your hand, you have made a cantilever.

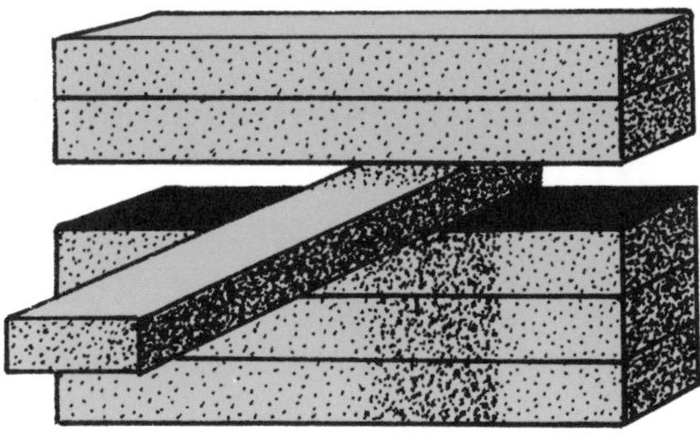

Materials for Graham Cracker Model

Waxed paper

Royal Icing (recipe page 97)

Box graham crackers

Spatula

Cardboard for base

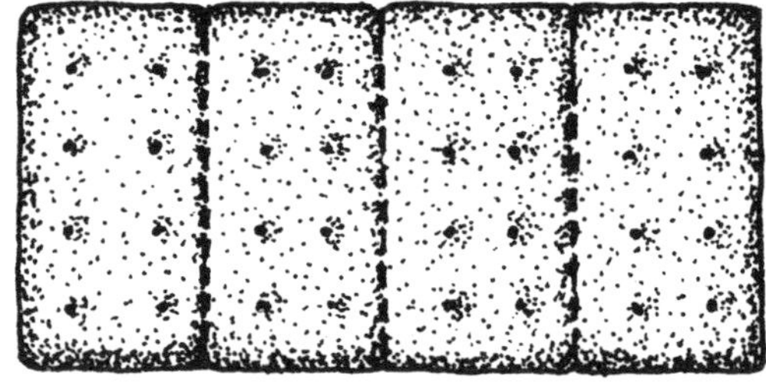

Materials for Foam Core Model

Sheet of foam core board

Exacto knife

Ruler

White glue or Royal Icing (recipe page 97)

Pencils

Cutting surface

❧ Graham crackers are a perfect size and shape for building cantilevers. You can build a model of Fallingwater using graham crackers and a cement called Royal Icing.

❧ Tear off a large piece of waxed paper and lay it down on a clean table. You will build your model on the waxed paper. If any icing drips down from your model, it will stick to the waxed paper instead of the table. When the model is finished, it will be easy to remove the waxed paper from the bottom. You will risk breaking the model if it dries stuck to the table.

❧ Practice building a cantilever with the graham crackers, so you will know how many crackers are needed to hold up a cantilever of one cracker.

❧ Now, looking at the picture of Fallingwater, build your model. When the model is finished, allow it to sit untouched for two hours in a dry place. This will give the Royal Icing a chance to dry. After you are finished admiring your model, you can eat it.

❧ Graham crackers will soon absorb the moisture in the air and your cantilevers will begin to sag. If you would like to make a permanent model, here is an easy way to do it.

❧ Count the number of graham crackers used in the model you made before. Trace the shape of a graham cracker on the foam core board and cut it out with an Exacto knife. Use this first rectangular shape as a pattern and cut out enough rectangles to make your model. Construct the model using white glue (which will require more patience and time to dry) or Royal Icing as cement. Cut a base from the remaining foam core board and cement your model to it.

Royal Icing

❧ Combine the sugar, egg whites, and cream of tartar in a mixing bowl and beat with an electric mixer set on low speed until the ingredients are blended together. If you like, you can add lemon juice for additional flavor. Then beat at high speed for 7 to 10 minutes. The icing is ready to use when you can draw a spoon or knife through it and the icing holds its shape.

❧ Royal Icing becomes very hard when it dries. Store it in a container with a tight-fitting cover.

Ingredients

3½ cups confectioners' sugar

2 egg whites

½ teaspoon cream of tartar

2 tablespoons lemon juice (optional)

Utensils

Electric mixer with bowl

Measuring spoons

Rubber spatula

Spoon or knife

Container with tight-fitting lid

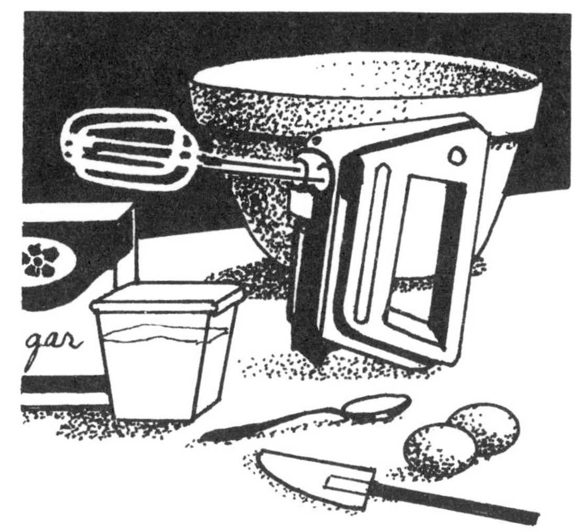

Materials

Worktable covered with newspaper or plastic

Aluminum foil baking pan, 8 by 3¾ by 2½ inches, one for each sculpture

Sand, 5-pound bag (gather at the beach or purchase at a pet or hardware store)

Water

Spatula

Tools for shaping sand (buttons, empty spools of thread, thimbles, forks, spoons, bottoms of glasses or other dishes and small pans, dice, balls, pencils, rulers, Lego blocks, Lincoln logs, screw drivers, nails, and pliers.)

Old bowl

Large old spoon

Bag of plaster, 5 pounds (purchase at a hardware store)

Old toothbrush or small paintbrush

MAKING A MODEL TEXTILE BLOCK FROM PLASTER

The geometric hollyhocks on the outside walls of the Hollyhock House were made or cast in a mold. The textile blocks were cast in a mold. Both hollyhocks and textile blocks are relief sculptures. We cannot see all sides of a relief sculpture because it is attached to a flat background. Relief sculptures may be carved by hand or cast in a mold. A mold is a space that has the negative shape of the sculpture.

The idea of positive and negative shapes is easier to understand in plane geometry. Drawing 1 shows a positive shape in white against a dark background. Drawing 2 shows the same shape as a negative, dark shape against a white background.

In solid geometry, the positive shape represents the sculpture. The negative shape represents the space into which the sculpture would fit exactly, or its mold.

1

2

❧ You can experiment with making relief sculptures in your own kitchen.

❧ Cover your worktable with newspaper or heavy plastic to protect it from your work materials. Fill the aluminum foil baking pan with 1 inch of sand.

❧ Wet the sand with enough water to make it firm, not soupy. If the sand is too dry, you will not be able to shape it. If it is too wet, your shape will sink back into the sand. Mix the sand thoroughly and smooth the top with a spatula until it is level.

❧ Use your tools to make a design in the sand. Press the tools firmly into the sand, but do not dig through to the bottom of the sand. If you dig through to the bottom, the plaster will run through and spoil your sculpture.

❧ Smooth the surface of the sand and try other designs. Look at the pictures of the hollyhocks (page 87) and textile blocks. Just for fun, try to recreate one in the sand. When you have made a design that pleases you, it is time to mix the plaster.

❧ Plaster is mixed in the proportion of 2 cups of water to 3 cups of plaster. To make a small batch, put 2 cups of water in the bowl and add 3 cups of plaster. Do not put the plaster in the bowl before the water because the plaster will not mix properly. Quickly stir the mixture until there are no lumps.

❧ Carefully dribble the plaster into the deepest places in your design. When they are filled, dribble—do not pour—the plaster over the sand until it is completely covered. If the plaster begins to harden, throw it away and mix a new batch. Do not try to thin the plaster by adding more water.

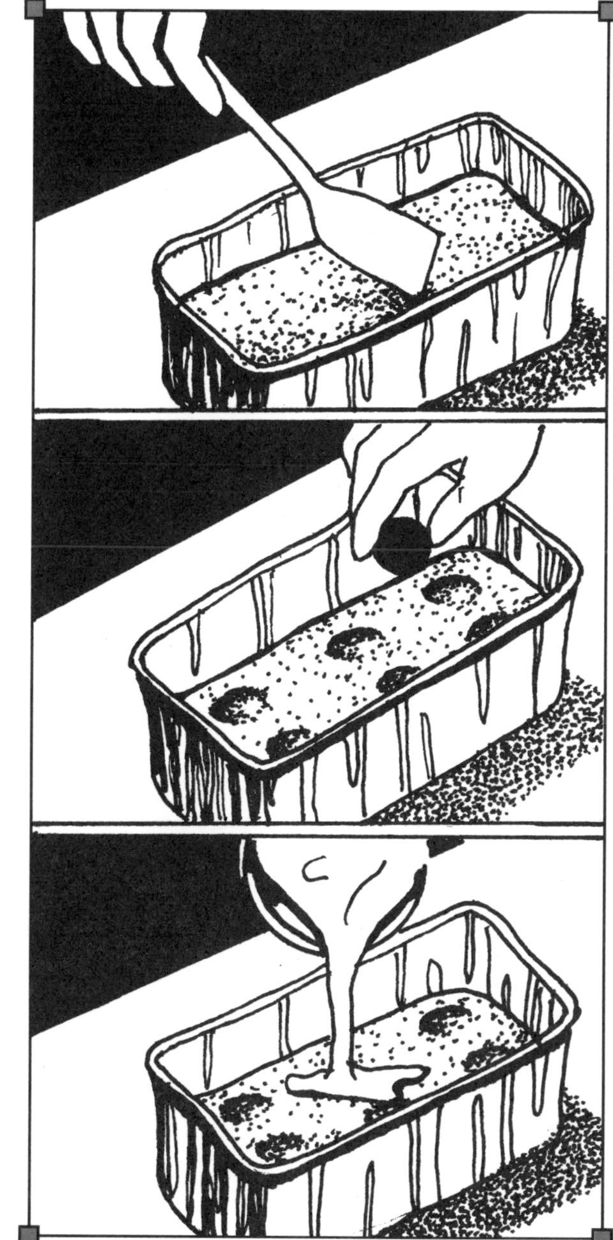

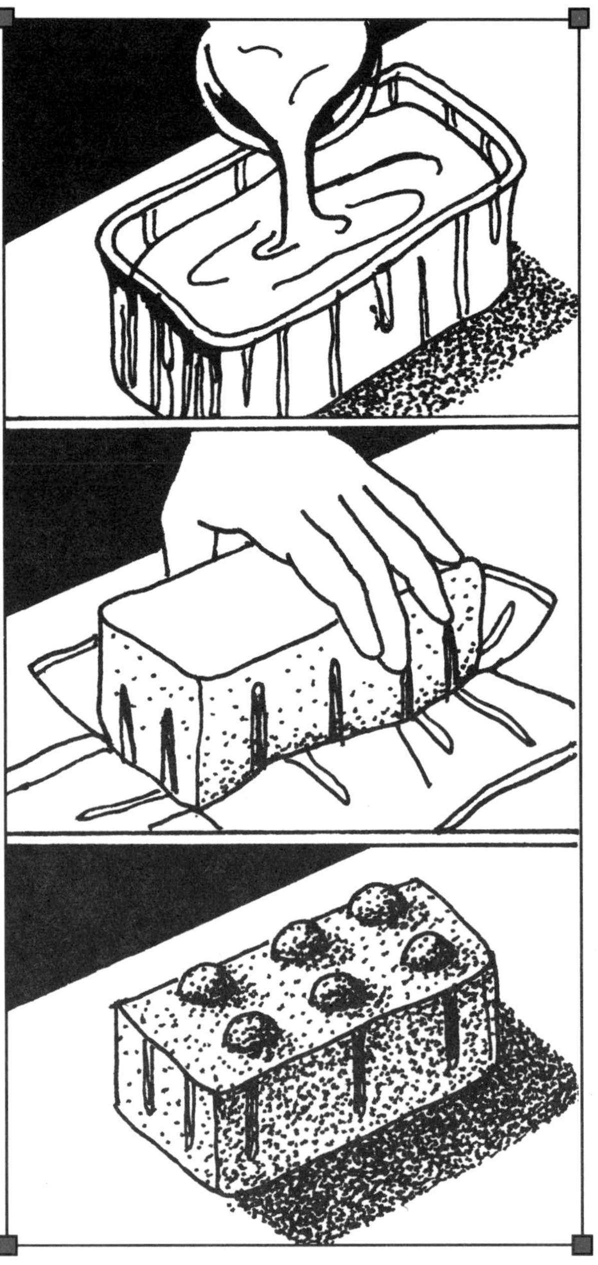

❧ When the sand is completely covered with dribbled plaster, you may gently pour the plaster into the mold. Pour plaster in the mold until the ½-inch space at the top is filled. Level the top with your spatula. If the first batch of plaster did not fill your mold completely, it is all right to mix a second batch and pour it into the mold as long as the sand is completely covered with the first batch.

❧ It will take about an hour for your mold to dry. During that hour, the plaster will harden and feel cold to the touch, then it will feel warm. When the plaster feels cold a second time, you can turn your sculpture out of the mold. Cut down the corners of the pan and peel the sides away. Carefully turn your mold out onto a piece of newspaper. Let the mold dry for another half an hour and gently brush off the excess sand with the toothbrush. As you brush, your design will begin to appear. Gather up the excess sand and save it to use again.

❧ It will take your sculpture several days to dry completely. As it dries, the sculpture will become lighter in weight, and the sand will become lighter in color. Until the plaster is completely dried out, a few grains of sand will come off when you touch your sculpture. When it is completely dry, no more sand will rub off.

LISTENING FOR SOUNDS MADE BY WATER

❧ *Frank Lloyd Wright thought of his organic houses as a meeting place for the four elements: earth, air, fire, and water. Perhaps water is the most interesting because it takes many different shapes. For example, water is the only element we can find as a solid, a liquid, and a gas in the earth's atmosphere at the same time. If this seems impossible to you, imagine yourself on a humid day, standing next to a swimming pool holding a glass filled with ice cubes. The humidity, pool, and ice are all different forms of water. Humidity is water as a gas; the pool is water as a liquid; and the ice is water as a solid.*

❧ *When Frank Lloyd Wright first visited the waterfall on Bear Run, he heard the music made by nature in the sound of falling water. If you close your eyes and think of the sound a waterfall makes, it is easy to understand why. Have you ever really thought about the sounds—or music—water makes in nature?*

❧ There are two lists in the box. The first one is a list of water words. The second is a list of words that describe sounds made by water. Fold a piece of lined paper in half to divide the lined spaces into two columns. Write the water words in the left-hand column, skipping a line between each word. Now write in a word in the right-hand column that makes you think of the sound made by the water word. Continue on down the list of water words, matching a sound to each word. Since some water words have many sounds, you may want to use some of the words more than once. Remember that music has rests or silent places. When you are listening for music in nature, think of silence as a part of nature's music.

Water Words	***Water Sounds***
waterfall	bubbling
icicle	pounding
ice	silent
snow	hissing
frost	cracking
fog	tinkling
rain	splashing
surf	crunching
stream	raging
hail	pattering
waves	lapping
cloud	dripping
geyser	pouring
river	rushing
brook	babbling
run	sprinkling

WORKING A CROSSWORD PUZZLE

❧ *You learned all of the words in this crossword puzzle while you read the story of Frank Lloyd Wright's life. If you need help remembering the words, the page number where the word appears is given as a hint. Rather than writing in this book, photocopy the puzzle and write your answers on that copy. Hint: the glossary in the beginning of this book will help you.*

Across

2. An object in the ceiling that lets sunlight into a room. (Hint: page 42)

5. This building material is an important part of modern buildings. In 1906, Frank Lloyd Wright was the first architect to use it as the main building material for a large building. (Hint: page 42)

8. A part of a building that extends out from the building in the same way a tree branch extends out from the trunk of a tree. (Hint: page 55)

9. An open porch with a roof over it that is often found along the sides of a Victorian house. (Hint: page 16)

10. The last name of the creator of Frank Lloyd Wright's favorite childhood building blocks. (Hint: page 2)

11. The nickname for Frank Lloyd Wright's woven concrete blocks. (Hint: page 50)

Down

1. In the early 1900s, the main living areas of most houses were divided into many little rooms. Frank Lloyd Wright's houses were different because the main living area had one large space just like the great American ________ spaces. (Hint: page 17)

3. A private place to sit next to the fireplace. (Hint: page 20)

4. A part of a Victorian house that rises up way beyond the roof. People can usually walk up into it and see for a great distance. (Hint: Page 16)

6. Another word for fireplace. (Hint: page 44)

7. The word Frank Lloyd Wright used to describe the way he designed his houses to be in perfect harmony with nature. (Hint: page 16)

1 2 3 4 5 6 7 8 9 10 11

SPACES

BLOCKS

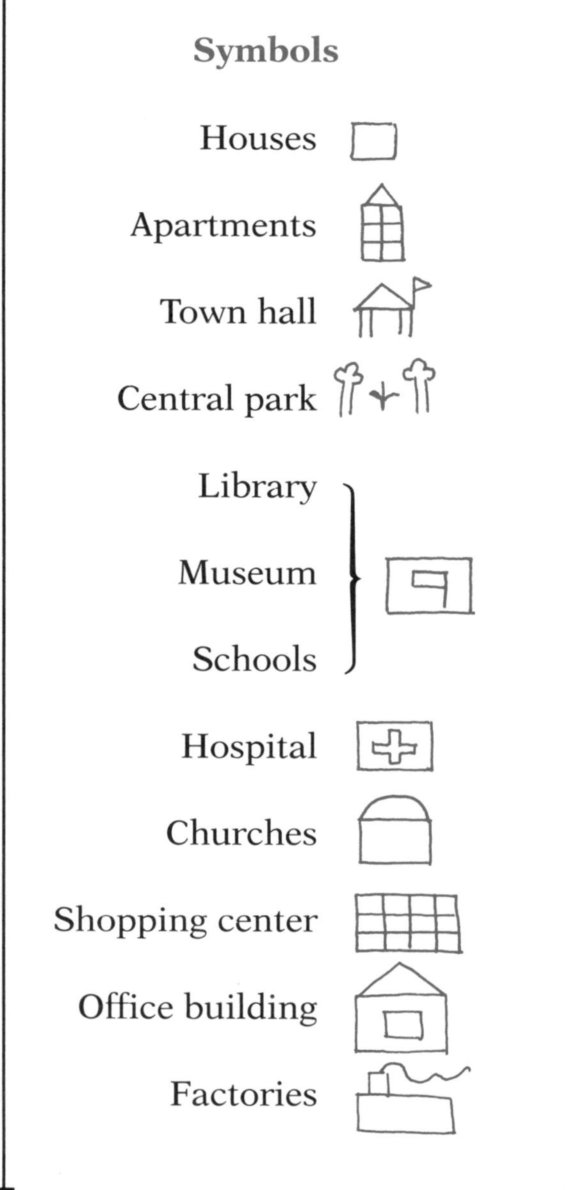

DESIGNING A CITY

As Frank Lloyd Wright grew older, he began to worry about the crowded American cities. He thought every family needed to have open space around them. With the help of his students, he developed a plan for Broadacre City, an imaginary place where there would be no crowding. Families would live happier lives on small farms where they would be close to nature.

Have you ever played with an electric train? When you laid down the track did you plan a place for a tunnel, a bridge, and a station? Did you also think about the farms, factories, and houses your train would pass on its journey around your room? When you stood up and looked at your train layout from above, you were looking at it in the same way an architect or city planner looks at a plan view. This is also the same way we look at a map.

In a plan view, all of the buildings, trees, and roads are shown with different geometric symbols. Using simple geometric shapes, you can plan an imaginary city on paper in the same way. First, you need to decide what buildings you want in your city. It should have houses and apartment buildings for people to live in. It should also have public buildings—places where people can get together to learn, work, play, shop, and worship. On the left is a list of buildings and symbols that are usually found in a small American city. Since this is probably the first time you have tried to design a city, it is a good idea to choose only a few items from the list.

❧ Your city must also have transportation or a way for the people who live there to travel around. Bicycles, motorcycles, cars, trucks, buses, and trains are some of the ways people who live in cities travel from place to place. When you plan your city, you will need to make a path for transportation.

❧ Geometric shapes are an easy way to show where the different places in your city can be found on a plan view. For example, houses can be shown with small squares and a roadway or train tracks with parallel lines. The symbols will give you some ideas of how to show buildings in a plan view.

❧ Before you begin planning your city, you will need to tape four sheets of graph paper together to make one big sheet. Tape the big sheet of graph paper to the table with drafting tape. After you lay out all of your supplies on the table, you are ready to begin.

❧ Imagine that you are in an airplane flying over a large piece of open land. It may be flat or hilly. It may be dry desert land or green prairie. Where will you put the roads and buildings? Where are the trees and parks? Where will people live?

❧ Before architects draw finished designs on paper, they sketch out their ideas on tracing paper. If you have a pad of tracing paper, tape a sheet of it over the graph paper and use it to sketch out your plan. You may erase or choose to use a new sheet of tracing paper over the first one as you plan your city. When the design is finished, draw the design carefully on the graph paper using a ruler and the template. Now you may color your drawing.

Materials

Clear tape

Several sheets blue line graph paper, 5 squares to the inch

Clean desk or flat work surface

Drafting tape

Small pad tracing paper (optional)

Several sharp 2H drawing pencils

Eraser

Ruler

Small architectural template (These are very inexpensive and may be purchased at an art or stationery store)

Assorted colored pencils

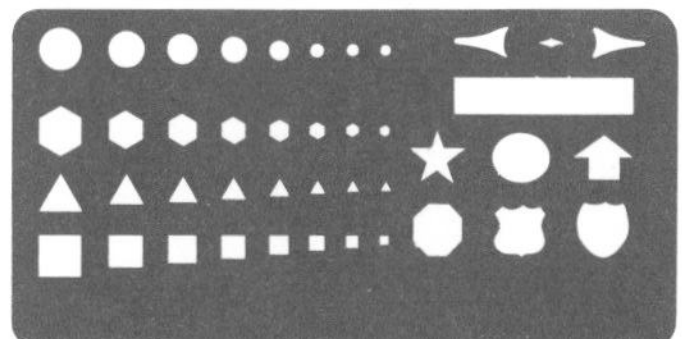

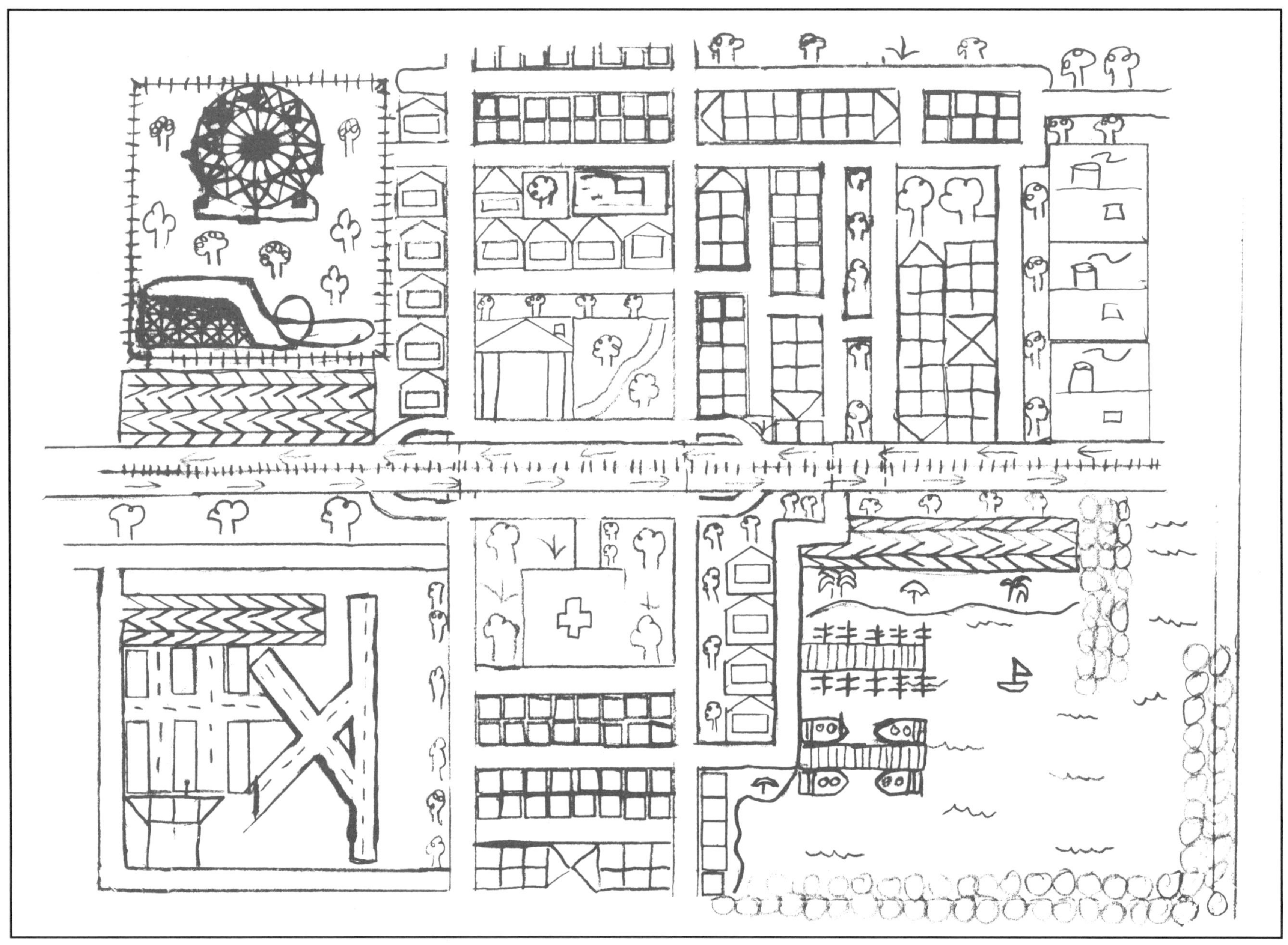

FINDING HEXAGONS IN NATURE

Almost all houses are made from square shapes. Because Frank Lloyd Wright tried out new ideas, he experimented with making houses from non-square shapes. Perhaps his most interesting non-square houses were the hexagonal houses.

He saw the shape of regular six-sided hexagons inside bee hives. Bees make their honey storage places in this shape because the hexagon is nature's best way of making a storage space. Frank Lloyd Wright thought nature's best way of making a storage space would also be the best way of using space for family living.

Since all the angles in a hexagon are greater than the angles in a triangle or square, there is more room to store things in the corners. This is why bees make their hives from hexagon shapes. Perhaps the reason that only a few of these unusual hexagonal houses were built is it is very difficult to match the many sides of many hexagons together perfectly. Anyone who has stitched a grandmother's flower garden quilt—a pattern made from tiny hexagons—knows how hard it is to match enough of these six-sided shapes together to cover a bed.

Oyster or soup crackers are usually made in the shape of small regular hexagons, and they are an easy way for you to experiment with making shapes from hexagons.

Materials

Oyster or soup crackers

White cardboard

White glue

Paints and a paintbrush

Materials

Pipe cleaners, any color

Old scissors

Drinking straws, or cocktail straws if you can find them (clear or a solid color will look best)

Worktable

White glue

Tissue paper, any color you like

- Spill some of the crackers out on the board and play with them until you have made a design that pleases you.
- Dab a small amount of glue to the back of each cracker and press it firmly in place on the cardboard. Allow to dry. Now you may paint your design if you wish.

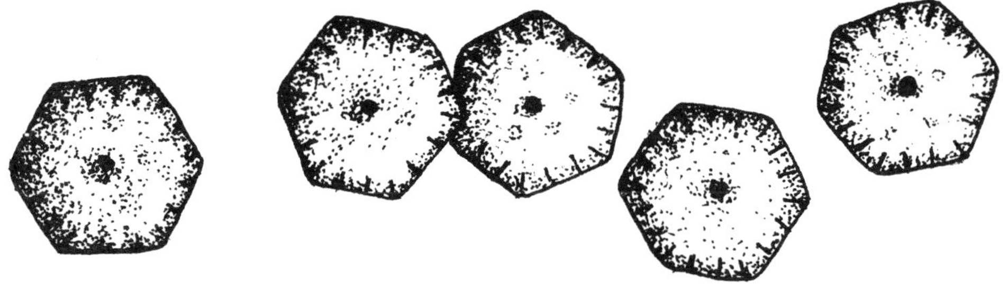

- Now try building your own hexagon shapes.
- Spill the pipe cleaners and drinking straws out onto the table.
- Cut the pipe cleaners and straws exactly in half. Bend the pipe cleaners in half and use them to join the drinking straws together into the shapes of hexagons. When you have made a design that pleases you and one that has symmetry—when one side of a line drawn down the center is exactly the same as the other side—run a small line of glue all along the straws and a dab at each joint. Place a sheet of tissue paper over your design and press down to join the glue with the straws. Allow time to dry. Cut around the outer edge of your shape.
- Make your design into a kite by adding a string and a tail.

❧ This drawing shows a pattern made from circles that are all the same size. The circles are drawn so all of their sides exactly touch each other. There is no extra space between them. Although the circles have no corners, there is wasted space in all the places where the circles come together.

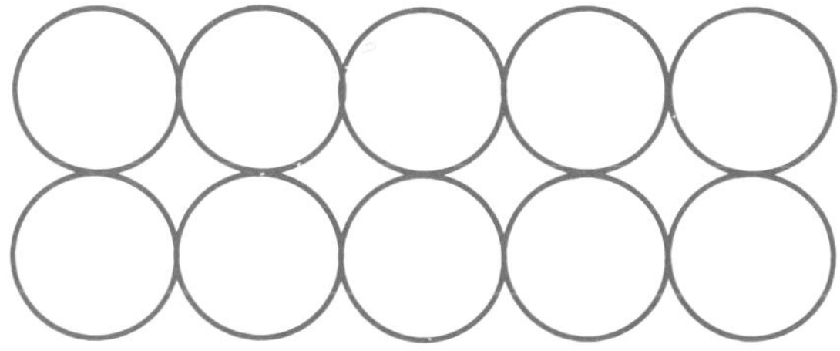

❧ This drawing shows a pattern of triangles of the same size. Half are turned upside down to make them fit closer together. Although there is no wasted space between triangles, the angles formed where the sides of the triangles meet are very small. Imagine what it would be like if your bedroom were triangle-shaped. Would your bed or dresser fit in the corners of the triangle?

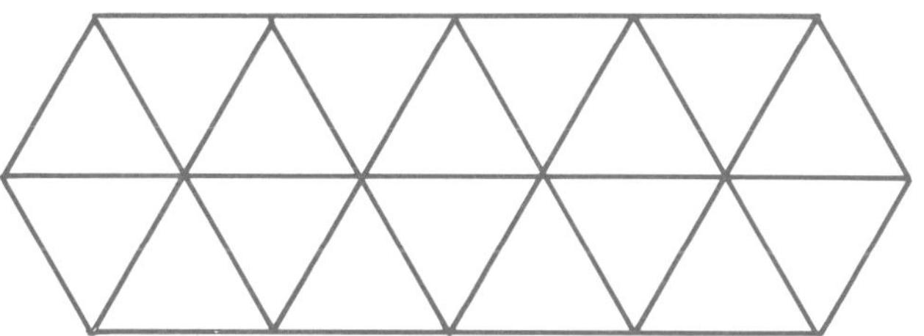

❧ This drawing shows a pattern made from squares. The squares fit together easily, and the angles formed where the sides meet are bigger than the angles formed by the triangles. Your room probably has square corners. Will the bed, desk, or dresser fit in the corners of your room?

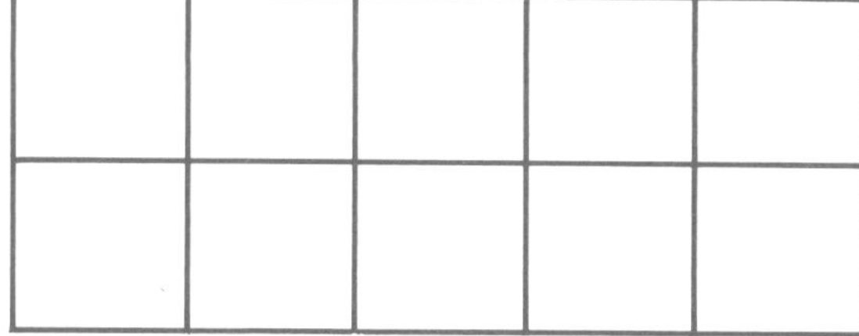

❧ This drawing shows a pattern of hexagons. The spaces formed where the sides of the hexagons meet are much bigger than the corner spaces formed by the triangles or the squares. If your room were shaped like a hexagon, it would be easy to fit the bed, desk, or dresser in the corners.

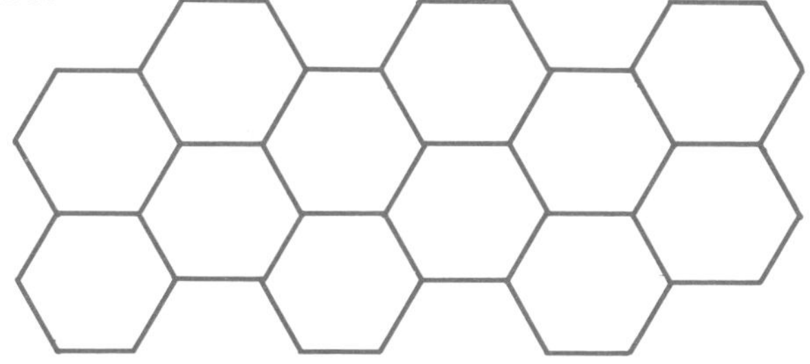

PLANNING SEASONAL FESTIVALS

❧ *Frank Lloyd Wright was a hard worker, but when his work was finished, he loved to have a good time. He gave big parties that reminded him of the happy Lloyd Jones Sunday family festivals of his childhood. The students of the Taliesin Fellowship sometimes worked for days preparing decorations, costumes, and food for Frank Lloyd Wright's celebrations. Music and a poem or a reading from one of his favorite books were also parts of the celebrations.*

❧ This activity gives you ideas about music, poetry, food, drink, and table decorations that will help you plan your own small seasonal festival. Check with your parents to arrange a time. Perhaps you could decorate the table and help prepare the dessert for a special family dinner. Maybe you could invite 2 or 3 friends over for an afternoon party. These seasonal festivals can be celebrated during the quiet times of the year when there are no birthdays or holidays. You can substitute the poems for your favorite poems or stories. If you do, try to pick some music to go along with it.

Spring Festival

❧ *Russian composer Modest Moussorgsky's music called "Night on Bald Mountain" and "Claire de Lune" by French composer Claude Debussy will paint musical pictures that will help you imagine the following humorous poem.*

❧ *Serve Strawberry Swirl with orange spice tea with milk and sugar.*

❧ *A basket filled with tall green grass is a perfect decoration for a spring table. Girls will have fun making party hats.*

The Wind and the Moon

Said the Wind to the Moon, "I will blow you out;
You stare in the air
Like a ghost in a chair,
Always looking what I am about—
I hate to be watched; I'll blow you out."

The Wind blew hard, and out went the Moon.
So, deep on a heap
Of clouds to sleep,
Down lay the Wind, and slumbered soon,
Muttering low, "I've done for that Moon."

He turned in his bed; she was there again!
On high in the sky,
With her one ghost eye,
The Moon shone white and alive and plain.
Said the Wind, "I will blow you out again."

The Wind blew hard, and the Moon grew dim.
"With my sledge, and my wedge,
I have knocked off her edge!
If only I blow right fierce and grim,
The creature will soon be dimmer than dim."

He blew and he blew, and she thinned to a thread.
  "One puff more's enough
  To blow her to snuff!
One good puff more where the last was bred,
And glimmer, glimmer, glum will go the thread."

He blew a great blast, and the thread was gone.
  In the air nowhere
  Was a moonbeam bare;
Far off and harmless the shy stars shone—
Sure and certain the Moon was gone!

The Wind he took to his revels once more;
  On down, in town,
  Like a merry-mad clown,
He leaped and halloed with whistle and roar—
"What's that?" The glimmering thread once
  more!

He flew in a rage—he danced and he blew;
  But in vain was the pain
  Of his bursting brain;
For still the broader the Moon-scrap grew,
The broader he swelled his big cheeks and blew.

Slowly she grew—till she filled the night,
  And shone on her throne
  In the sky alone,
A matchless, wonderful silvery light,
Radiant and lovely, the queen of the night.

Said the Wind: "What a marvel of power am I!
  With my breath, good faith!
  I blew her to death—
First blew her away right out of the sky—
Then blew her in; what strength have I!"

But the Moon she knew nothing about the affair;
  For high in the sky,
  With her one white eye,
Motionless, miles above the air,
She had never heard the great Wind blare.

—George Macdonald

Strawberry Swirl

❧ Wash the fresh berries carefully, removing the stems and the berries that are soft and squishy. Pick out the 4 best-looking berries and set them aside to use later for decorations. Place the rest of the berries in the blender and blend until the berries are a liquid. Add the sugar and blend enough to mix it in.

❧ Empty half the package of gelatin into a small bowl and pour the boiling water over it. Stir until the gelatin is dissolved. Add the gelatin to the strawberries and mix. Refrigerate the strawberry and gelatin mixture for half an hour.

❧ Whip the cream with an electric mixer until stiff peaks form when the beaters are lifted from the bowl.

❧ With a rubber spatula, gently fold the strawberries into the whipped cream. Make streaks and swirls of pure cream and berries by not completely mixing the two together. Spoon it into the glass parfait dishes and decorate with the berries you set aside before. Refrigerate one hour before serving.

❧ Makes 4 servings.

Ingredients

1 box fresh, ripe strawberries
½ cup sugar
1 package unflavored gelatin
¼ cup boiling water
1 cup (pint) whipping cream

Utensils

Blender
Plastic or metal measuring cups
Small bowl
Tea kettle
Electric mixer with bowl
Rubber spatula
4 glass parfait dishes

Ingredients

Water

2 orange spice tea bags

1 cup milk

Sugar cubes

Utensils

Tea kettle

Teapot

Tea cozy or dish towel

Small saucepan

Hot pads

4 teacups

Orange Spice Tea with Milk and Sugar

❧ Fill the tea kettle with cold water and bring the water to a boil.

❧ Fill the teapot with boiling water and let it warm the pot for a minute or two. Pour the water back in the tea kettle and bring the water to a boil again.

❧ Put the tea bags in the teapot and fill it with boiling water. Cover the teapot with a tea cozy or a dish towel and let the tea steep for about 5 minutes.

❧ While the tea is steeping in the teapot, warm milk in the small saucepan, or you may use a microwave to heat the milk.

❧ Fill each teacup half full of milk and then fill the rest of the cup with tea. Serve the tea with sugar cubes.

❧ Makes 4 servings.

A Basket of Spring Grass

You can grow thick, healthy grass in less than a week from wheat seeds. The supplies you will need are usually sold at feed stores and nurseries. If you have trouble finding either of them, you can substitute rye grass seed and potting soil.

Line the basket with plastic wrap. Fill it with vermiculite leaving a 2-inch space at the top to put the seed. Sprinkle the wheat seed on top of the vermiculite.

Set the basket in a sink and add water until the seed feels moist. You will not need to water it again for at least a week.

Set the basket on a pan in a warm place where it will get filtered sunlight. To keep the wheat seed moist, cover the basket loosely with plastic wrap. Remove the plastic wrap after 2 days. The seeds should take a few more days to grow.

Materials

Large basket or bowl-shaped flower pot

Heavy plastic wrap

1 pound vermiculite or potting soil

1 pound wheat seed or rye grass seed

Large pan

Materials

Old straw hat

1–2 yards 1-inch ribbon

Scissors

6–12 small floral vials

Fresh spring wild or garden flowers with stems

Assorted green leafy plants with stems

12 pieces florists wire

Spring Party Hat

❧ *Most of the women who attended Frank Lloyd Wright's Easter celebrations wore hats that they decorated themselves. Here is an easy way for you to make an unusual spring hat.*

❧ Ask a parent or another adult to help you remove any old decorations from the hat.

❧ Trim the flower stems to about 6 inches. Fill the floral vials with water and put one or two flowers in each one.

❧ Tie the ribbon around the brim of the hat. The ribbon can hang down over the brim of the hat or it can be tied in a bow and arranged on top.

❧ Arrange the flower-filled vials around the brim and fasten them to the hat with the florists wire. Stick a few green leafy plants into the vials and spread them out to cover plastic vial.

❧ Any extra flower-filled vials can be inserted in the basket of spring grass and used to decorate the table.

Summer Festival

❧ *Composer Ferde Grofé's "On the Trail" from his Grand Canyon Suite mimics the sound of mules trotting along the canyon walls. Lewis Carroll's nonsense poem, "The Walrus and the Carpenter" from* Through the Looking Glass *tells us about a very unusual summer walk along the beach around the time of the summer solstice. Play this music and imagine how oysters would sound trotting along behind the Walrus and the Carpenter in the following poem.*

❧ *Serve cream puffs, filled with sweetened whipped cream, and pink lemonade.*

❧ *Decorate your summer table with garden flowers and colorful origami pinwheels.*

The Walrus and the Carpenter

The sun was shining on the sea,
    Shining with all his might:
He did his very best to make
    The billows smooth and bright—
And this was odd, because it was
    The middle of the night.

The moon was shining sulkily,
    Because she thought the sun
Had got no business to be there
    After the day was done—
"It's very rude of him," she said,
    "To come and spoil the fun!"

The sea was wet as wet could be,
    The sands were dry as dry.
You could not see a cloud, because
    No cloud was in the sky:
No birds were flying overhead—
    There were no birds to fly.

The Walrus and the Carpenter
    Were walking close at hand:
They wept like anything to see
    Such quantities of sand:
"If this were only cleared away,"
    They said, "it would be grand!"

"If seven maids with seven mops
  Swept it for half a year,
Do you suppose," the Walrus said,
  "That they could get it clear?"
"I doubt it," said the Carpenter,
  And shed a bitter tear.

"O Oysters, come and walk with us!"
  The Walrus did beseech.
"A pleasant walk, a pleasant talk,
  Along the briny beach:
We cannot do with more than four,
  To give a hand to each."

The eldest Oyster looked at him,
  But never a word he said:
The eldest Oyster winked his eye,
  And shook his heavy head—
Meaning to say he did not choose
  To leave the oyster-bed.

But four young Oysters hurried up,
  All eager for the treat:
Their coats were brushed, their faces washed,
  Their shoes were clean and neat—
And this was odd, because, you know,
  They hadn't any feet.

Four other Oysters followed them,
  And yet another four;
And thick and fast they came at last,
  And more, and more, and more—
All hopping through the frothy waves,
  And scrambling to the shore.

The Walrus and the Carpenter
  Walked on a mile or so,
And then they rested on a rock
  Conveniently low:
And all the little Oysters stood
  And waited in a row.

"The time has come," the Walrus said,
  "To talk of many things:
Of shoes—and ships—and sealing wax—
  Of cabbages—and kings—
And why the sea is boiling hot—
  And whether pigs have wings."

"But wait a bit," the Oysters cried,
"Before we have our chat;
For some of us are out of breath,
And all of us are fat!"
"No hurry!" said the Carpenter.
They thanked him much for that.

"A loaf of bread," the Walrus said,
"Is what we chiefly need:
Pepper and vinegar besides
Are very good indeed—
Now, if you're ready, Oysters dear,
We can begin to feed."

"But not on us!" the Oysters cried,
Turning a little blue.
"After such kindness, that would be
A dismal thing to do!"
"The night is fine," the Walrus said,
"Do you admire the view?"

"It was so kind of you to come!
And you are very nice!"
The Carpenter said nothing but
"Cut us another slice.
I wish you were not quite so deaf—
I've had to ask you twice!"

"It seems a shame," the Walrus said,
"To play them such a trick.
After we've brought them out so far,
And made them trot so quick!"
The Carpenter said nothing but
"The butter's spread too thick!"

"I weep for you," the Walrus said:
"I deeply sympathize."
With sobs and tears he sorted out
Those of the largest size,
Holding his pocket-handkerchief
Before his streaming eyes.

"O Oysters," said the Carpenter,
"You've had a pleasant run!
Shall we be trotting home again?"
But answer came there none—
And this was scarcely odd, because
They'd eaten every one.
—Lewis Carroll

Ingredients

1 cup water

½ cup butter

¼ teaspoon salt

1 cup all-purpose flour

4 extra-large eggs

1 batch sweetened whipped cream (recipe page 121)

Powdered sugar

Berries or sliced fresh fruit

Utensils

2-quart heavy saucepan

Glass measuring cup

Plastic or metal measuring cups

Measuring spoons

Wire whisk

Ungreased cookie sheet

Timer

Hot pads

Cooling rack

Spatula

Cream Puffs

❧ This recipe makes 12 to 16 large cream puffs. The total baking time is 35 minutes. The oven is set at 450° for the first 10 minutes and then is turned down to 400° for 25 minutes.

❧ Before mixing the ingredients, preheat oven to 450°.

❧ Measure water in a glass measuring cup and pour it into the saucepan. Bring it to a boil. Be careful not to allow the water to boil away on stove; if it does, the cream puffs will not rise.

❧ Add butter and salt to boiling water and stir until dissolved.

❧ When the water begins to boil again, gradually beat in the flour with a wire whisk. Continue beating the mixture until it pulls away from the sides of the pan.

❧ Remove the pan from the stove and beat in the eggs one at a time. Keep beating until the batter is smooth, stiff, and glossy.

❧ Scoop the batter out in large spoonfuls onto the ungreased baking sheet leaving about 3 inches between mounds of batter.

❧ Place the baking sheet in the center of the oven and set the timer for 10 minutes. When the timer goes off, turn the oven temperature to 400°. Set the timer for 25 minutes.

❧ When the timer goes off the second time, the cream puffs should be a beautiful golden brown color. Remove them from the oven and transfer them from the baking sheet to a cooling rack with a spatula.

❧ When the cream puffs are cool, cut in half and fill with sweetened whipped cream. Sprinkle with powdered sugar. Serve the cream puffs on a pretty plate with fresh berries or slices of fresh fruit.

Sweetened Whipped Cream

❧ *Real cream was one of Frank Lloyd Wright's favorite treats. When he was a boy, he always wished to be given cream instead of milk as a reward for a hard day's work on the farm. His thrifty family churned every drop of cream into butter and there was never any left for the young Frank.*

❧ Pour the cream into a bowl and beat until stiff with an electric mixer.

❧ Slowly mix in the powdered sugar and vanilla.

Whipped Cream Ingredients
1 cup heavy cream
2 tablespoons powdered sugar
1 teaspoon vanilla

Utensils
Electric mixer with bowl
Measuring spoons

Pink Lemonade

❧ Combine the lemon juice, water, syrup, and sugar and stir until the sugar dissolves. Pour the lemonade into ice-filled glasses. You may garnish the glasses with a thin slice of fresh lemon.

❧ Makes 4 servings.

Lemonade Ingredients
½ cup lemon juice
3 cups water
¼ cup maraschino cherry syrup
½ cup sugar
Ice cubes
Lemon, sliced (optional)

PINWHEEL ❧ Step 1

Beginning with the white side of the paper up, fold and crease as shown below. Open the paper and lay it flat on the table, white side up.

❧ Step 2

Fold both sides to the center and crease.

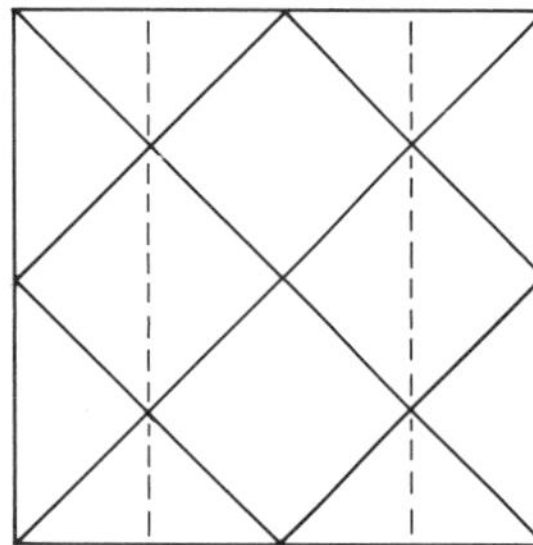

❧ Step 3

Fold both sides to the center and crease, making a small square.

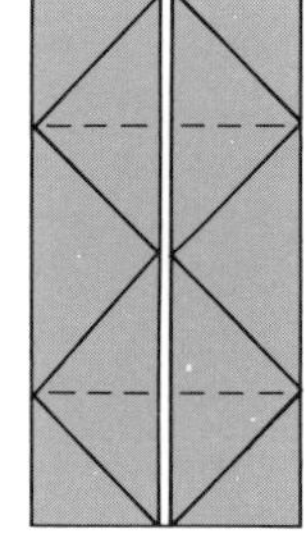

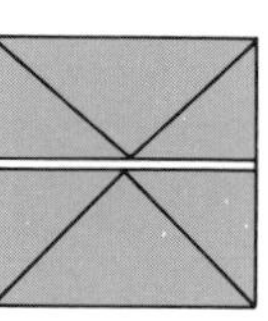

❧ Step 4

Lay folded paper square on the table with loose flaps on top. Lift the right upper flap away from the table and pull corner out.

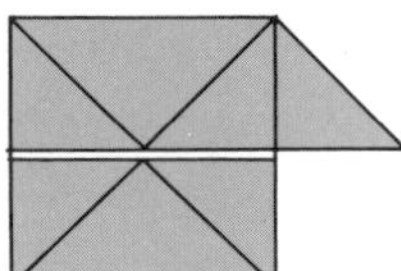

❧ Step 5

Repeat Step 4 on the remaining three corners.

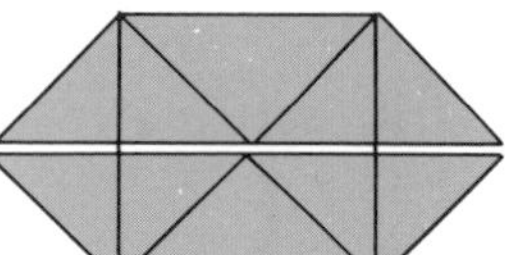

❧ Step 6

Lay the folded paper on the table. Fold the upper right-hand flap up. Burnish between thumb and first finger to hold in place. Fold the remaining 3 flaps in the same way. This is the origami windmill shape.

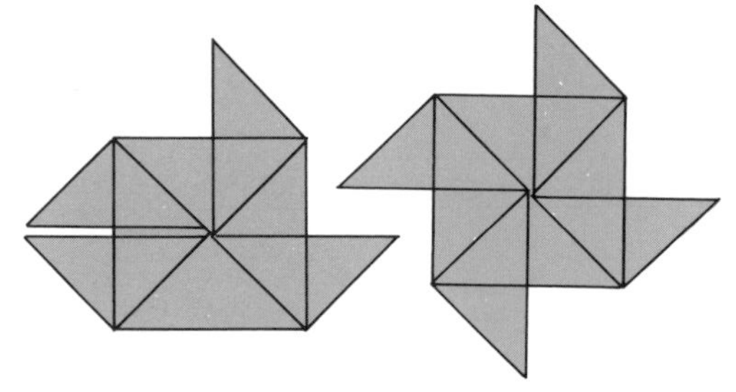

Origami Pinwheels

❧ Fold the pinwheels as shown on page 122.

❧ You may want to have an adult help you assemble the pinwheels. Tear off a small piece of clear tape and stick it to the center with the point of the cotter pin. Remove the pin.

❧ With a heavy, sharp needle, pierce a hole through both sides of the clear drinking straw approximately ¼ inch from one end. Force the cotter pin through both holes in the straw. Pass the cotter pin through the hole in the center of the windmill and, using the pliers, open the sides of the cotter pin enough to hold the windmill in place on the drinking straw.

Materials

6 pieces colored origami paper (6 by 6 inches)

Clear tape

Clear drinking straws

Large sharp needle

6 fine cotter pins, ¾ inch long

Needle-nose pliers

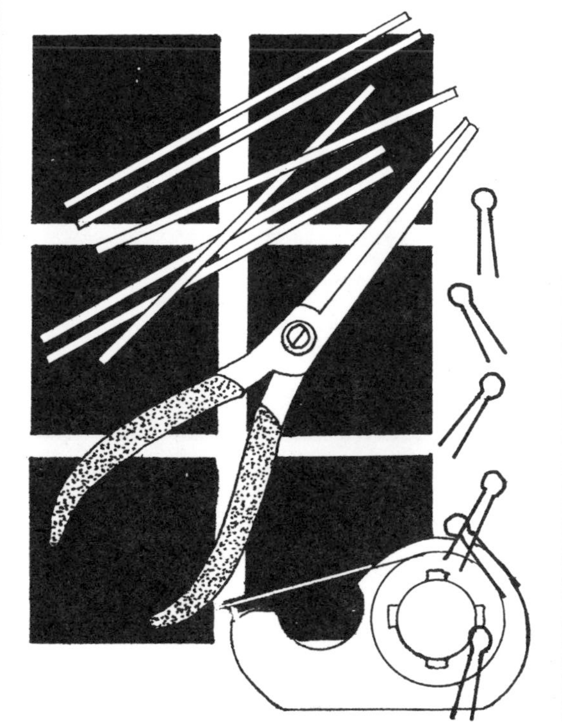

Fall Festival

❧ *"Pictures at an Exhibition" by Russian composer Modest Moussorgsky will help you imagine the pictures painted by "Jack Frost."*

❧ *Frank Lloyd Wright designed Taliesin, his home in Wisconsin, to help nature create frozen water sculptures in the winter. The following poem describes the frozen winter scenes nature made on the Taliesin windows.*

❧ *Serve cinnamon muffins and hot spiced apple cider with a stick of cinnamon in it.*

❧ *A colorful autumn table can be decorated with apples, small pumpkins, squash, nuts, and dried leaves. Dry the leaves in warm sand before you put them on the table.*

Jack Frost

The door was shut, as doors should be,
Before you went to bed last night;
Yet Jack Frost has got in, you see,
And left your window silver white.

He must have waited till you slept;
And not a single word he spoke,
But penciled o'er the panes and crept
Away again before you woke.

And now you cannot see the hills
    Nor fields that stretch beyond the lane;
But there are fairer things than these
    His fingers traced on every pane.

Rocks and castles towering high;
    Hills and dales, and streams and fields;
And knights in armor riding by,
    With nodding plumes and shining shields.

And here are little boats, and there
    Big ships with sails spread to the breeze;
And yonder, palm trees waving fair
    On islands set in silver seas.

And butterflies with gauzy wings:
    And herds of cows and flocks of sheep;
And fruit and flowers and all the things
    You see when you are sound asleep.

For creeping softly underneath
    The door when all the lights are out,
Jack Frost takes every breath you breathe,
    And knows the things you think about.

He paints them on the window pane
    In fairy lines with frozen stream;
And when you wake you see again
    The lovely things you saw in dream.

—Gabriel Setoun

Ingredients

Butter for greasing muffin tin

¼ cup melted butter

1 extra-large egg

½ cup milk

1½ cups all-purpose flour

2¼ teaspoons baking powder

¼ teaspoon salt

⅓ cup white sugar

½ teaspoon nutmeg

Topping

⅓ cup melted butter

1 teaspoon cinnamon

⅓ cup white sugar

Utensils

Muffin pan

Small saucepan

Mixing bowls

Glass measuring cup

Plastic or metal measuring cups

Measuring spoons

Flour sifter

Cooling rack

Hot pads

Rubber spatula

Cinnamon Muffins

❧ This recipe makes 10 to 12 muffins. Baking time is approximately 12 minutes and the preheated oven temperature is 425°.

❧ Grease the muffin pan generously with butter.

❧ Set all ingredients and utensils out on a clean working space.

❧ Melt ¼ cup butter in a saucepan over a low flame on the stove. You may also melt the butter in a bowl in a microwave.

❧ Break the egg into a small bowl and beat it with a fork until the white and yolk are thoroughly combined.

❧ Measure the milk by pouring it into the glass measuring cup, setting the cup on the table, and checking the measurement at eye level. Stir the milk into the beaten egg.

❧ Measure the melted butter in the glass measuring cup and stir it into the egg and milk mixture.

❧ Measure the flour, baking powder, salt, sugar, and nutmeg and sift them together into the medium-sized bowl.

❧ Make a small hole in the center of the flour mixture and pour the egg, milk, and butter mixture into it.

❧ With the mixing spoon, stir only enough to wet all of the flour mixture. Muffin batter should be lumpy.

❧ Spoon equal amounts of batter into the well in the muffin pan. Place the pan in the middle of the oven and bake.

❧ Prepare the topping while the muffins are baking. Melt ⅓ cup butter in a small saucepan. Mix the cinnamon and sugar in a small bowl. Set both the saucepan and bowl on the table.

❧ The muffins are done when the tops are golden brown. Remove the muffins from the pan and cool them on a rack for a few minutes. When the muffins are cool enough to touch, dip the top of each muffin first in the butter and then in the sugar and cinnamon mixture.

❧ Serve the warm cinnamon muffins in a basket that has been lined with a pretty dish towel.

Hot Spiced Apple Cider

Ingredients

1 quart apple juice or cider

6–8 whole cloves

6 sticks cinnamon

¼ cup sugar

Pinch nutmeg

Utensils

Plastic or metal measuring cups

Medium saucepan

Strainer

❧ Combine all the ingredients except 4 sticks of cinnamon in a saucepan and simmer for 10 minutes. Save the extra cinnamon sticks for garnish.

❧ Pour the spiced cider through a strainer into the mugs. Serve hot.

❧ Makes 4 servings.

Materials

Sand, 5-pound bag

Large metal pan

Assorted well-shaped, colored leaves

Electric heating pad

Dried Autumn Leaves

- Pour a ¼-inch layer of sand over the bottom of a clean metal pan and smooth it with your hand.
- Carefully arrange the leaves on the smooth sand without overlapping any parts of the leaves.
- Cover the leaves with another ¼-inch layer of sand.
- Plug in the heating pad and turn the dial to low. Place the pan on the pad for three days.
- Carefully remove the leaves from the sand. You may save the sand to use again.

Winter Festival

❧ *Claude Debussy wrote a collection of short piano pieces for children called the "Children's Corner Suite." The fourth and fifth pieces, "The Snow Is Dancing" and "Golliwogs Cakewalk," will help you imagine the scene in the following poem of dancing potatoes on a winter evening. Another beautiful piece of music that accompanies prancing potatoes and a cold night is "Pavane" by Gabriel Faure. It is easy to imagine the druid priests singing this tale to children in the early days of the British Isles.*

❧ *Serve geometric shape cookies with hot white chocolate.*

❧ *If your parents have white dishes and a white table cloth, it will be fun to set an all-white winter table decorated with glittering snowflakes.*

The Potatoes' Dance

I

"Down cellar," said the cricket,
"Down cellar," said the cricket,
"Down cellar," said the cricket,
"I saw a ball last night,
In honor of a lady,
In honor of a lady,
In honor of a lady,
Whose wings were pearly white.
The breath of bitter weather,
The breath of bitter weather,
The breath of bitter weather,
Had smashed the cellar pane.
We entertained a drift of leaves,
We entertained a drift of leaves,
We entertained a drift of leaves,
And then of snow and rain.
But we were dressed for winter,
But we were dressed for winter,
But we were dressed for winter,
And loved to hear it blow.
In honor of the lady,
In honor of the lady,
In honor of the lady,
Who makes potatoes grow,
Our guest the Irish lady,
The tiny Irish lady,
The airy Irish lady,
Who makes potatoes grow.

II

"Potatoes were the waiters,
Potatoes were the waiters,
Potatoes were the waiters,
Potatoes were the band,
Potatoes were the dancers
Kicking up the sand,
Kicking up the sand,
Kicking up the sand,
Potatoes were the dancers
Kicking up the sand.
Their legs were old burnt matches,
Their legs were old burnt matches,
Their legs were old burnt matches,
Their arms were just the same.
They jigged and whirled and scrambled,
Jigged and whirled and scrambled,
Jigged and whirled and scrambled,
In honor of the dame,
The noble Irish lady
Who makes potatoes dance,
The witty Irish lady,
The saucy Irish lady
Who makes potatoes prance.

III

"There was just one sweet potato
He was golden brown and slim.
The lady loved his dancing,
The lady loved his dancing,
The lady loved his dancing,
She danced all night with him,
She danced all night with him.
Alas, he wasn't Irish
So when she flew away,
They threw him in the coal-bin,
And there he is today,
Where they cannot hear his sighs
And his weeping for the lady,
The glorious Irish lady,
The beauteous Irish lady,
Who
Gives
Potatoes
Eyes."

—Vachel Lindsay

Geometric Shape Cookies

- This recipe will make four dozen small cookies. Baking time is 8 to 10 minutes, and the preheated oven temperature is 350°.
- Lightly grease the cookie sheets with the extra butter.
- Measure butter and put it in a large mixing bowl. Beat with an electric mixer until butter is fluffy and light in color.
- Measure sugar, add it to butter, and beat for 1 or 2 minutes.
- Add egg to the mixing bowl and beat just enough to mix in.
- Measure vanilla and cream and beat them into mixture.
- Sift flour, baking powder, and salt together and gradually add to mixture in the bowl.
- When all the flour is mixed into the dough, cover bowl tightly with plastic wrap and refrigerate for 1 hour.
- Divide dough into four equal balls. Place dough, one ball at a time, on lightly floured pastry cloth. Sprinkle a little flour on top of dough and roll it out to about ⅛ of an inch thick. If you lift the rolling pin slightly as you reach the edge, the dough will not crack or split on the edges.
- Cut cookies in geometric shapes and carefully transfer them to a cold, lightly greased baking sheet. Bake only one baking sheet of cookies in the oven at a time.
- Bake in a 350° oven for 8 to 10 minutes until cookies are a light brown around the edges. Remove the baking sheet from the oven and let cookies cool for 5 minutes before moving them from the baking sheet to a cooling rack with a spatula.
- You may roll your dough scraps a second and third time.

Ingredients

Butter or margarine for greasing the cookie sheets

1 cup butter

1 cup sugar (white or brown)

1 extra-large egg

1 teaspoon vanilla

2 tablespoons cream

3 cups all-purpose flour

1 teaspoon baking powder

⅛ teaspoon salt

White Buttercream Frosting (recipe page 132)

Nonpareils (for decoration)

Utensils

2 cookie sheets

Plastic or metal measuring cups

Electric mixer with mixing bowl

Measuring spoons

Rubber spatula

Rolling pin and pastry cloth

Cooling rack

Hot pads

Ingredients

4 tablespoons melted butter

1 teaspoon vanilla

1 tablespoon lemon juice

1-pound box sifted powdered sugar

Water or milk

Utensils

Small saucepan

Measuring spoons

Electric mixer with bowl

Rubber spatula

Table knife

White Buttercream Frosting

- Melt the butter in a small saucepan.
- Mix the melted butter, vanilla, lemon juice, and sugar in a small mixing bowl until the frosting is smooth. If the frosting is too stiff, add a small amount of water or milk to make it thin enough to spread on the cookies.
- When the cookies are no longer warm to the touch, they may be frosted. Put the nonpareils (either white or multicolored) in a small bowl and press the frosted cookies into them before the frosting hardens.

Hot White Chocolate

❧ Measure milk and pour it into the saucepan. Heat it over a low flame until bubbles begin to form around the sides of the pan. Add the white chocolate pieces, salt, honey, and vanilla and stir until they are dissolved. Pour the hot white chocolate into the mugs and top with marshmallows or whipped cream.

❧ Makes 4 servings.

Ingredients

4 cups milk

4 ounces white chocolate, ground into small pieces

Pinch salt

½ cup honey

1 teaspoon vanilla

Marshmallows or whipped cream

Utensils

Glass measuring cup

Plastic or metal measuring cups

Measuring spoons

Medium saucepan

Wooden spoon

Hot pads

4 mugs

Materials

12 large, round-shaped coffee filters that have been ironed flat

Scissors

Glitter spray glue

White glitter

Newspaper

Worktable

Paper Snowflakes

❧ Working with one coffee filter paper at a time, fold the paper in half and then fold it into thirds. Cut out the first snowflake following the pattern shown below. Then cut several patterns of your own.

❧ Place your snowflakes on a piece of newspaper and spray them with glitter glue. Immediately dust the snowflakes with iridescent white glitter.

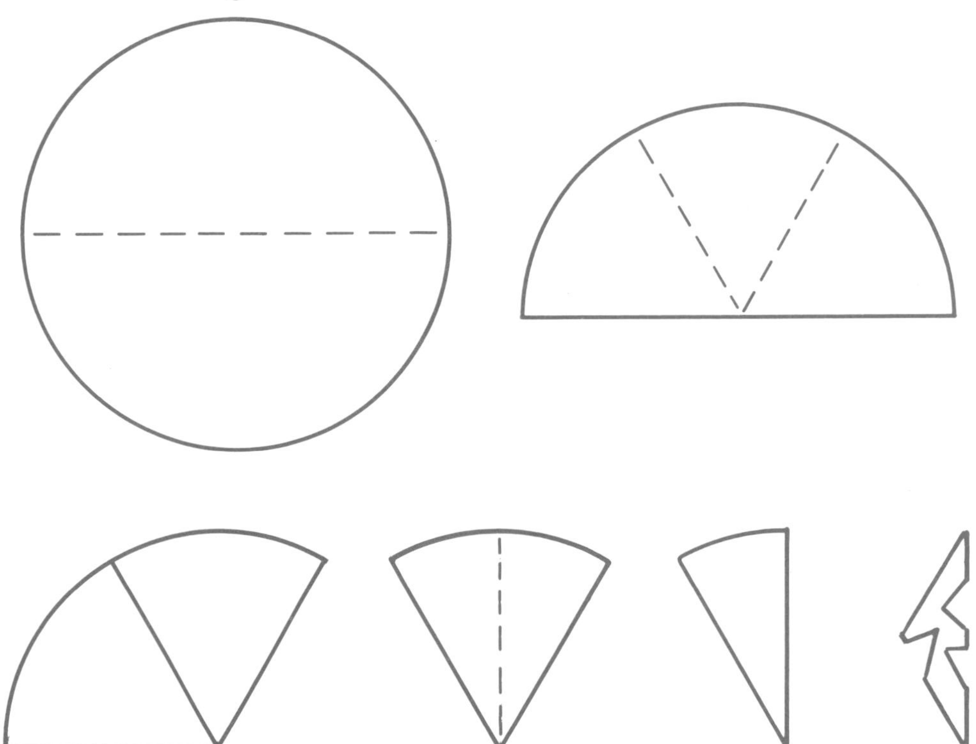

PLANNING A FIELD TRIP TO A FRANK LLOYD WRIGHT HOUSE

❧ *The best way to understand what a Frank Lloyd Wright house is really like is to visit one. Many of his houses are preserved as museums for all of us to visit, learn from, and enjoy. The following list will help you find the house nearest to you. Talk over the best way for you to visit one of these houses with your parents. Ask a parent's permission before making any phone calls.*

Northeastern United States

Fallingwater
PO Box R, Mill Run, PA 15464
(412) 329-8501

Built for the Kaufmann family in 1936, Fallingwater cantilevers over the waterfall on Bear Run. It is open daily in the summer and on weekends only in the winter. Reservations are required. Special children's tours are available by previous arrangement.

Isadore and Lucille Zimmerman House
192 Orange Street, Manchester, NH 03104
(603) 669-6144

This house was built in 1950 and combines Wright's prairie and usonian styles. Call or write for tour information.

Southern United States

Pope-Leighey House
PO Box 37, Mount Vernon, VA 22121
(703) 780-4000

An early usonian-style house built in 1940. Call or write for tour information.

Midwestern United States

Frank Lloyd Wright Home and Studio
951 Chicago Avenue, Oak Park, IL 60302
(708) 848-1500

Wright's first home and studio was built between 1889 and 1898. Daily tours are available year-round. Call or write for tour schedule.

Meyer May House
450 Madison Southeast, Grand Rapids, MI 49503
(616) 246-4821

This brick prairie house was built in 1908. Call or write for tour schedule.

Taliesin
Route 3, Spring Green, WI 53588
(608) 588-2511

Built between the years 1902 and 1925, this group of buildings was Wright's home and studio. Call or write for tour schedule.

Frederick C. Robie House
5757 South Woodlawn Avenue, Chicago, IL 60637
(312) 702-8374

The finest of the prairie houses, the Robie House was built in 1908. One tour is offered daily at noon. Call to confirm the tour time.

James Charnley House
1365 North Astor Street, Chicago, IL 60610
(312) 951-8006

Wright designed this small townhouse in 1891 while he was working as a draftsman. Call or write for tour schedule.

Dana-Thomas House
301 East Lawrence Avenue, Springfield, IL 62703
(217) 782-6776

Built in 1900, this is the largest of Wright's prairie houses and is a National Historic Landmark. Call or write for tour schedule.

Lowell Walter House
PO Box 1, Quasquenton, IA 52362
(319) 934-3572

Built on a bluff above the Wapispinicon River, this is a large group of buildings. Call or write for tour schedule.

Southwestern United States

Taliesin West
Cactus Road and 108th Street
Scottsdale, AZ 85261
(602) 860-2700

This was Wright's winter home and studio. It is now the home of the Frank Lloyd Wright School of Architecture. Call or write for tour schedule.

Hollyhock House
4808 Hollywood Boulevard, Barnsdall Park
Los Angeles, CA 90027
(213) 662-7272 or (213) 485-4581

A 1918 house set on a hilltop. Call or write for tour schedule.

Ennis-Brown House
2655 Glendower Avenue, Los Angeles, CA 90027
(213) 660-0607

A textile block house built in 1923–24. Call or write for tour schedule.

Samuel Freeman House
1962 Glencoe Way, Los Angeles, CA 90068
(213) 851-0671

A textile block house built in 1923–24. Call or write for tour schedule.

Bibliography

Barney, Maginel Wright. *The Valley of the God-Almighty Joneses: Reminiscences of Frank Lloyd Wright's Sister*. New York: Appleton-Century, 1965.

Blumenson, John. *Identifying American Architecture: A Pictorial Guide to Styles and Terms, 1600-1945*. New York: W. W. Norton & Co., 1981.

Connors, Joseph. *The Robie House of Frank Lloyd Wright*. Chicago: The University of Chicago Press, 1984.

Costantino, Maria. *Frank Lloyd Wright*. New York: Crescent Books, 1991.

Forsee, Aylesa. *Frank Lloyd Wright: Rebel in Concrete*. Philadelphia: Macrae Smith Company, 1959.

Forsee, Aylesa. *Men of Modern Architecture*. Philadelphia: Macrae Smith Company, 1966.

Gebhard, David. *Romanza: The California Architecture of Frank Lloyd Wright*. San Francisco: Chronicle Books, 1988.

Historic American Buildings Survey. *What Style Is It?: A Guide to American Architecture*. Washington, DC: The Preservation Press, 1983.

Hoffman, Donald. *Frank Lloyd Wright's Robie House: The Illustrated Story of an Architectural Masterpiece*. New York: Dover Publications, Inc., 1984.

Hoffman, Donald. *Frank Lloyd Wright's Fallingwater: The House and Its History*. New York: Dover Publications, Inc. 1978.

Kenneway, Eric. *Origami: Paperfolding for Fun*. London: Octopus Books, Ltd., 1980.

Murphy, Wendy Bueher. *Frank Lloyd Wright, Genius! The Artist and the Process*. Englewood Cliffs, New Jersey: Silver Burdett Press, 1990.

Naden, Corinne J. *Frank Lloyd Wright: The Rebel Architect*. New York: Franklin Watts, Inc., 1968.

Ravielli, Anthony. *An Adventure in Geometry*. New York: The Viking Press, 1957.

Russel, Solveig Paulsen. *Lines and Shapes: A First Look at Geometry*. New York: Henry Z. Walck, Inc., 1965.

Sergeant, John. *Frank Lloyd Wright's Usonian Houses*. New York: Whitney Library of Design, Watson-Guptill Publications, 1984.

Sitomer, Mindel and Harry. *What Is Symmetry?* New York: Thomas Y. Crowell Company, 1970.

Vakahama, Voshie. *The Joy of Origami*. Tokyo: Shufunotono/Japan Publications, 1985.

Willard, Charlotte. *Frank Lloyd Wright: American Architect*. New York: The Macmillan Company, 1972.

Wright, Frank Lloyd. *An Autobiography*. New York: Duell, Sloan and Pearce, 1943.

Wright, John Lloyd. *My Father, Frank Lloyd Wright*. New York: Dover Publications, Inc., 1992.

House Beautiful. June 1992, page 46.

Activity page answers:

Page 69: Solid geometric shapes, top row, left to right: cube, pyramid
bottom row, left to right: sphere, cone, cylinder
Regular polygons, top row, left to right: octagon, hexagon
bottom row, left to right: pentagon, nonagon, septagon
Regular polyhedrons, top row, left to right: octahedron, hexahedron or cube, tetrahedron
bottom row, left to right: icosahedron, dodecahedron
Page 71: Left to right: leaf, star, sailboat
Page 72: Triangle, American flag
Page 85: Doors: 7, steps: 10, windows: 19, trees: 5, shrubs, 18
Page 103: Across 2. skylight, 5. concrete, 8. cantilever, 9. veranda, 10. Froebel, 11. textile.
Down 1. open, 3. inglenook, 4. tower, 6. heart, 7. organic.

For photographs and illustrations I am grateful to the following:

Photograph on front cover, courtesy of Western Pennsylvania Conservancy/Fallingwater; on back cover, by Jon Miller © Hedrich-Blessing;

on page 1, courtesy of Frank Lloyd Wright Home and Studio Foundation Catalog, on pages 3 (H1090), 21 (H256A), 22 (H273), 24 (drawing by Maginel Wright Barney, H292), 26 (H254), and 30 (H87), courtesy of Frank Lloyd Wright Home and Studio Foundation;

on pages 4, 63 © Land's End, Inc., courtesy of Land's End Catalog;

on pages 7, 32, 56, and 62, courtesy of State Historical Society of Wisconsin;

on page 8, courtesy of Chicago Historical Society;

on pages 11 and 13, courtesy of Crombie Taylor, FAIA;

on pages 15, 34, 37, 38, 39, 50, 51, 55, 57, 77 (right), and 97, courtesy of Donald Hoffmann;

on page 16, courtesy of Pulliam Family;

on pages 18, 19, 25, and 27 courtesy of Jon Miller © Hedrich Blessing;

on page 23, courtesy of Harold Buchholz;

on page 31, courtesy of Lorraine Robie O'Connor;

on page 36, courtesy of Wasmuth Portfolio of 1910;

on page 40, courtesy of Jeannette Wilber Scofield;

on pages 41, 58, 77 (left), 78, and 79 (except for lower right), © Kathleen Thorne-Thomsen

on pages 42, 43, and 45, courtesy of the Museum of Modern Art, New York;

on pages 46 and 48, courtesy of the City of Los Angeles Cultural Affairs Department, Gift of David and Michael Devine;

on page 49 © Julius Shulman and on page 79 (lower right), © Julius Shulman, courtesy of James Pulliam, FAIA;

and on pages 54 and 59, courtesy of Pedro Guerrero.

Illustrations on front cover, pages 2, 14, 35, 52, 70, 87, 110, 111, 113–116, 121, 124, 125, 127, and 129–133 by Jennifer Koury;

on page iv by Anthony Hurtig;

on pages 5, 17, 19, and 29 by Linda Brownridge;

on pages 9, 14, 16 and 20 by Owen Smith;

on pages 9, 69, 71, 72, 85, 88–92, 105, 115, 122, 123, 128, and 134 by Kathleen Thorne-Thomsen;

on page 12 by Crombie Taylor, FAIA;

on pages 25 and 75, by Steelcase, Inc.;

on pages 61 and 85, by James Pulliam FAIA;

on pages 65, 66, 69, 73, 74, 76, 81, 93, 94, 95–100, 107, and 108 by Trudy Lucas;

on page 67 and 106 by Graham Pulliam;

on page 68 by Stuart Freed;

on page 73 by James J. Pulliam;

on page 112 by Heather Kortebien;

on pages 117, 118, and 119 by John Tenniel.

Designer: Kathleen Thorne-Thomsen

Typography: Jerry Robin, J. Robin & Associates, Pasadena, California. Composed using Quark Xpress 3.2 on a Macintosh FX. Type: New Aster with Futura heads.

Printed by Lammar Offset Printing, Hong Kong

Curr NA 737 .W7 T56 1994
Thorne-Thomsen, Kathleen.
Frank Lloyd Wright for kids